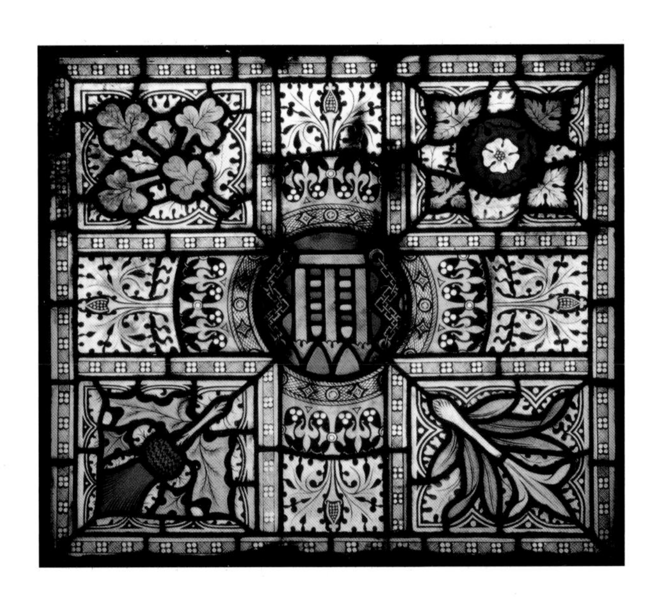

The Palace of Westminster

OFFICIAL GUIDE

HOUSES OF PARLIAMENT

Introduction

THE PALACE OF WESTMINSTER – HOME OF THE UK PARLIAMENT

The Palace of Westminster is one of the most recognisable buildings in the world. With Big Ben's Clock Tower at one end and the Victoria Tower at the other, its striking façade stretches for 287 metres alongside the River Thames.

From its beginnings in the 11th century, when Westminster Hall was used as a meeting place for the King and his Council, the Palace has evolved to become the workplace of a 21st century Parliament. Leaders of the nation and great men and women have spoken here, and continue to do so today. Here too, great historical figures have been condemned, bombs have fallen and laws which changed the world have been made.

The Palace's architecture reflects many of the changes that have taken place over the centuries, and the works of art and national treasures it contains echo many of the historic events it has witnessed.

Today, the Palace remains at the heart of the United Kingdom, home to its Parliament. Here, you can watch the House of Commons and House of Lords at work as they address the nation's most important issues.

This guide will introduce you to the buildings, their contents and their history. Visitors are welcome to Parliament and the Palace of Westminster, and the rooms and spaces featured in this guide are available to tour as part of your visit. You will find a wealth of detail online at *www.parliament.uk*, including information about how to plan your visit.

The Palace of Westminster
Michael Heseltine, oil on canvas, 1993 [WOA 3711]

The artist Canaletto was the first to popularise views of the Thames at Westminster during the 18th century, a trend that has been followed by artists ever since.

Frontispiece:
The stained glass, made by Hardman & Co, is part of a glazed ceiling in a House of Lords corridor leading to the west front of the building. It shows flowers representing the four historical parts of the UK: the rose for England, leek for Wales, thistle for Scotland and shamrock for Ireland around the royal motif of a crowned portcullis.

"We may be proud that England is the ancient country of Parliaments. With scarcely any intervening period, Parliaments have met constantly for 600 years, and there was something of a Parliament before the Conquest. England is the mother of Parliaments."

JOHN BRIGHT, British politician and orator, 1865

The term the 'Mother of Parliaments' is often associated with the Houses of Parliament, but Bright used it to refer to England. He was describing the model of democratic government that the country had developed over the centuries, and which has been followed by many countries around the world.

History

The Palace of Westminster is a site of immense historical and cultural significance in the national life of the United Kingdom. The view of the Clock Tower rising above the magnificent Gothic Revival palace is instantly recognisable as a symbol of the nation.

A royal palace has existed here for nearly a thousand years, and has been Parliament's home for about half that time. Charles Barry designed the buildings in their current form in the mid-19th century and much of what we see today is just over 150 years old. Some parts, however, are much older, going back to the times when English kings and queens lived here.

FIRST BUILDINGS

Little trace remains of the original 11th century royal palace, although there was such a building near Westminster Abbey from at least the reigns of Canute (d. 1035) and Edward the Confessor (d. 1066). Yet one extraordinary structure does survive, albeit modified, from the 1090s – King William Rufus's (1056-1100) colossal hall, which is now called Westminster Hall.

With this, the largest royal hall in Europe, Westminster became the English monarch's principal residence, but the medieval palace was not only home to the royal family. The offices of the government, including the Exchequer – the Treasury's predecessor – and the law courts also came to be based here. It was also often the meeting place for the assembly of magnates which, by the early 13th century, was sometimes called 'parliament'.

THE BEGINNINGS OF PARLIAMENT

Parliament developed from councils of leading men – barons and bishops – called together by the king to advise him on how to rule. These meetings go back at least as far as the Anglo-Saxon 'Witan' (from the Old English word 'witenagemot' for 'meeting of wise men') which operated from before the 7th century until the 11th century.

Relations between the king and magnates often became a struggle for power and influence. In 1215, a group of them forced King John (1167-1216) to recognise that there were limits to the monarch's authority. The result of this, the Magna Carta, is the first great constitutional document in English history. This was the first time an English monarch formally recognised that his subjects had proper legal rights, such as the right not to be condemned without trial.

At first, Parliament met wherever the king happened to be, but from the early 14th century it usually met at Westminster. The last time Parliament met outside the capital was the Oxford Parliament of 1681.

What is Parliament?

The word 'parliament' comes from the Old French word *parlement* or discussion: when kings needed advice, they would summon certain people to discuss important issues such as war, taxation and the law, and to help them govern. Today, the Westminster Parliament is composed of three parts: the House of Commons, the House of Lords and the Sovereign. The Commons is the assembly of representatives known as MPs (Members of Parliament) elected to represent constituencies throughout England, Scotland, Wales and Northern Ireland.

It is difficult to tell exactly when the 'first' Parliament happened because, although medieval kings organised various meetings of important people, not all would have been recognisable to us as a Parliament; for example, they did not include representatives from all parts of England. During the 13th century, kings began to summon representatives of the counties ('knights of the shire') and of the towns ('burgesses') to Parliaments as well as the magnates. The Parliament assembled by Simon de Montfort (*c.* 1208-1265) in January 1265, to which both knights and burgesses were summoned, is sometimes seen as the first to have had the main elements of a modern Parliament. In particular, it discussed matters of broad political concern, not just taxation.

The Lords and the Commons later began to sit in separate rooms or chambers, the Commons sometimes meeting in the Chapter House or the Refectory (dining hall) of the neighbouring Abbey.

THE MEDIEVAL PALACE

In the 13th century, the Palace of Westminster was enlarged under Henry III (1207-72), and royal apartments were built for the king (the Painted Chamber, so called because of its remarkable wall paintings) and queen. The most significant development was the building of St Stephen's Chapel between 1292 and 1348. The chapel was intended to rival the gothic Sainte-Chapelle in Paris which had been commissioned by Louis IX of France earlier in the 13th century. Work on a lower chapel for the royal household began in 1292, and on an upper chapel for the royal family, in 1320. The lavish decoration of both was completed in 1363.

The Painted Chamber, 1799
William Capon, watercolour, 1817 [WOA 1648]

King Henry III's richly coloured wall paintings with scenes taken from the Old Testament had disappeared from view under coats of limewash by the time of this painting; instead the room is hung with tapestries illustrating the Trojan War.

King John Assents to Magna Carta
Charles Sims, oil on canvas, 1927 [WOA 2602]

King John
John Thomas and the Thames Bank Workshop
Stone, *c.* 1854 [WOA S148]

St Stephen's Chapel
G Earp
Oil on canvas, *c.* 1880
[WOA 2257]

This reconstruction captures the richly painted and gilded decoration of the medieval chapel. The main figures are King Edward III and Queen Philippa.

Few of the Palace's medieval buildings survive. The most significant surviving structure is Westminster Hall's vast wooden roof. The roof was constructed under Richard II (1367-1400), who remodelled the Hall between 1393 and 1401 into the form it takes today. The walls were heightened and reinforced, the huge windows installed, and an entrance with two castle-like towers resembling an abbey was built. Various embellishments were added, including the statues of kings which remain in the Hall to this day. The Jewel Tower from Edward III's (1312-77) palace, built around 1365, and located near Westminster Abbey, also survives.

HOME OF PARLIAMENT

After a major fire at Westminster in 1512, Henry VIII (1491-1547) left the Palace, eventually taking over an adjoining palace which became known as Whitehall. It occupied the area to the north of Parliament that now houses government departments and Downing Street. The Palace of Westminster became a warren of administrative and legal offices. Over the years, numerous extensions and modifications turned the whole area into a maze of decaying structures.

Soon, the Palace of Westminster had become the recognised home of the two Houses of Parliament. The Lords normally sat in the Queen's Chamber, which it occupied until 1801. In 1547, Edward VI (1537-53) gave permission for the Commons to sit in the by then disused St Stephen's Chapel, which remained its home until a devastating fire in 1834 destroyed nearly all of the medieval palace.

The Jewel Tower was built in the mid-14th century to house Edward III's treasures. At that time, it was known as the King's Privy Wardrobe. It was later used to store parliamentary documents. It is not part of the parliamentary estate, but can be visited by the public and stands between the Palace of Westminster and Westminster Abbey.

North West View of the Jewel Tower
John Thomas Smith
Etching, 1805 [WOA 4501]

The Great Roof
Frank O Salisbury, 1924
Oil on canvas [WOA 2730]

King Richard II and his Master Carpenter Hugh Herland are shown inspecting the construction of the great roof of Westminster Hall in 1397. The massive medieval timbers are accurately drawn, as the artist was given special access to the scaffold which had been erected in the Hall in the early 1900s to carry out remedial work.

Speaker Lenthall Asserting the Privileges of the Commons against Charles I when the Attempt was made to seize the Five Members, 1642
Charles West Cope
Waterglass [WOA 2894]

Speaker Lenthall (1591-1662) famously resisted Charles I when he was told to identify MPs the King wanted to arrest, saying: *"May it please your majesty, I have neither eyes to see nor tongue to speak in this place but as this House is pleased to direct me whose servant I am here; and humbly beg your majesty's pardon that I cannot give any other answer than this to what your majesty is pleased to demand of me."*

St Stephen's Chapel occupied almost the same space as St Stephen's Hall does today. Its interior structure of a narrow room with two sets of facing benches has been the model for the Chamber of the House of Commons ever since. Supporters of the Government sit to the Speaker's right and Opposition MPs sit to the left.

From early on, Parliament had its own staff – the first Clerk of the Parliaments, the most senior member of the House of Lords' administration, was appointed in 1315 and the House of Commons appointed its first Clerk in 1363 – and many of them lived on the parliamentary estate. The daily manuscript journals kept by the clerks survive as far back as 1510 for the Lords and 1547 for the Commons. The House of Lords' records were stored in the Jewel Tower, where they survived the fire of 1834; the House of Commons' records were kept elsewhere in the Palace and most of them were burnt. Parliament's archives are still kept on site, in a purpose-built repository in the Victoria Tower.

Manuscript Journal of the House of Lords, 1510.

Parliamentary Archives, HL/PO/JO/1/1

Manuscript Journal of the House of Commons, 5 November 1605 recording the discovery of the Gunpowder Plot.

Parliamentary Archives, HC/CL/JO/1/5

THE GUNPOWDER PLOT

The Palace of Westminster was almost destroyed on 5 November 1605. The Gunpowder Plot is the name given to the conspiracy to blow up the Houses of Parliament and the king, James I (1566-1625), during the State Opening of Parliament. The gunpowder was discovered beneath the Lords Chamber the night before and the plot failed. The anniversary is still marked with bonfires and fireworks, and a ceremonial inspection of the Palace's cellars takes place before the monarch arrives for the State Opening of Parliament.

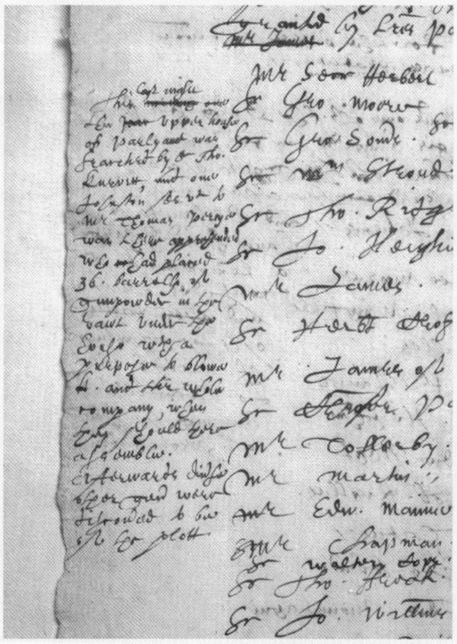

Gunpowder Plot – The Principal Conspirators 1605
Crispijn van der Passe
Engraving [WOA 1349B]

The Flight of the Five Members, 1642
John Seymour Lucas
Oil on canvas, 1915
[WOA 2953]

PARLIAMENT AND THE CIVIL WAR

In one of the most dramatic parliamentary occasions, Charles I (1600-49) came to the Commons on 4 January 1642. He arrived with a group of soldiers to try to arrest five MPs who were his political enemies. Parliament became the focus for opposition to the king. This complex struggle led to the Civil War, Charles I's trial in Westminster Hall and execution in 1649, and the Interregnum until 1660, when no monarch was on the throne. Since that time, no monarch has entered the House of Commons Chamber, with one exception. George VI had a private tour of the rebuilt Chamber after the Second World War with his daughters, the future Queen Elizabeth II and her sister Princess Margaret.

The Mace was traditionally a weapon, a heavy club or truncheon, but in the Middle Ages it became a symbol of authority, acquiring embellishment and ceremonial use on the way. The Mace must be present for sittings of either House to be lawful. The Lords have two maces (though only one is used at a time) and the Commons one.

Devolution: Scotland and Ireland had their own Parliaments from the 13th century until the Acts of Union of 1707 and 1800 which created the United Kingdom. After the partition of Ireland in 1921, Northern Ireland had its own Parliament until 1973. Welsh constituencies started to send MPs to Westminster in 1542, six years after Wales was constitutionally united with England in 1536. The modern Scottish Parliament, Welsh Assembly and Northern Ireland Assembly were all established by Acts of Parliament (pictured above and kept in the Parliamentary Archives) passed in 1998. While all parts of the United Kingdom elect MPs to the House of Commons to ensure that their interests are represented at Westminster, matters that are specifically Scottish, Welsh or Northern Irish ('devolved matters') are decided in those assemblies. Policy areas such as foreign policy and defence remain the responsibility of the Westminster Parliament, and are known as 'reserved matters'.

Oliver Cromwell (1599-1658) was one of the leading parliamentarians in the struggle against Charles I, but he too failed to manage the unruly Commons. In a climactic scene in 1653, he lifted up the Mace, which he described as 'a fool's bauble', and brought the Parliament to an end.

Early Parliaments met at irregular intervals. They started to meet every year in more or less regular sessions lasting several months after the Glorious Revolution of 1688 finally established Parliament's supremacy over the monarchy. This development of Parliament into a permanent institution brought pressures to bear on the building. Maintenance and the lack of space were never adequately addressed, although changes were occasionally made.

Oliver Cromwell
Hamo Thornycroft, bronze [WOA S29]

Debate raged for over 50 years about whether to erect a statue of Cromwell, until finally in the 1880s Thornycroft's over-life size bronze was commissioned. Funded by an anonymous benefactor, who was later revealed as the former Prime Minister Lord Rosebery, the statue was positioned prominently in a garden outside Westminster Hall.

THE FORMATION OF THE UNITED KINGDOM

In 1707, the Commons had 513 Members, including 24 from Wales, which first sent MPs to the Parliament at Westminster in 1542. Following the Act of Union with Scotland in 1707, 16 Scottish peers joined the Lords, which still had a comparatively small membership of about 200, and another 45 MPs joined the Commons.

The Commons Chamber was altered to accommodate them, even though it had recently undergone substantial renovation in 1692 under the guidance of Christopher Wren (1632-1723).

The House of Commons in Session
Peter Tillemans, oil on canvas, c. 1710 [WOA 2737]

The debating Chamber is shown shortly after the Act of Union with Scotland, with Speaker Onslow in the Chair. It is one of the earliest paintings of the House of Commons and resembles the original layout of the chapel, with Members sitting on pews facing one another.

Articles of Union between England and Scotland, 22 July 1706.

Parliamentary Archives, HL/PO/JO/10/6/106/2307

After the 1800 Act of Union with Ireland, 100 Irish MPs joined the Commons, bringing the total to 658, and an extra row of benches was inserted on each side of the Chamber. At the same time, the House of Lords, which had now grown to about 300, including 32 Irish peers and bishops, moved into a bigger Chamber, the Lesser Hall, that had once held a law court called the Court of Requests.

Even after its move, the interior of the House of Lords in the old Palace of Westminster was similar to that of the Commons. One major difference was that the Lords had Cross Benches set at right angles to the sides of the Chamber and facing the Lord Chancellor on the Woolsack. Sir John Soane (1753-1837) designed new State Apartments in neo-classical style and added a new royal entrance and gothic-style façade in the mid-1820s.

PARLIAMENT AND POLITICS IN THE 18TH CENTURY

From the 18th century, the Commons began to exert greater control over financial matters – the raising of taxes and spending of public money. Eventually, this led to the Commons becoming the dominant House. Over time, the monarchy also came to play a less significant role in the process of government; the last royal veto over legislation was used by Queen Anne (1665-1714) in 1708 on the Scottish Militia Bill.

The 18th century saw the emergence of the office of Prime Minister, a parliamentarian who chaired a small Cabinet and acted as head of the Government. Robert Walpole (1676-1745) established the role through his expertise in financial affairs and ability to retain a majority of supporters in the Commons. There were periodic outbursts of opposition in Parliament, but national political parties evolved slowly and the current system involving two or three main parties developed during the 19th century.

The 18th and 19th centuries were an age of great parliamentary oratory. William Pitt the Elder (1708-78) and his son, William Pitt the Younger (1759-1806), both served as Prime Minister, as did Lord Palmerston (1784-1865), William Ewart Gladstone (1809-98) and Benjamin Disraeli (1804-81). Other great statesmen of the time who were renowned for their oratory include Charles James Fox (1749-1806), Edmund Burke (1729-97) and George Canning (1770-1827) who also served briefly as Prime Minister. These and many other parliamentarians are depicted in sculptures and paintings in Parliament.

A Recent Escape
Isaac Cruikshank, etching, 1795
[WOA 6794]

William Pitt the Younger's military failure made him unpopular and the repressive measures he introduced were fiercely attacked by his great political rival Charles James Fox. Political satires of the two men were popular during the late 18th century; here they are shown as characters from Shakespeare's *Macbeth*. William Pitt the Younger, his clothes spattered with mud, blames an unrepentant Charles James Fox for his predicament.

An 18th century visitor to the Palace of Westminster wrote in 1736 that *"'tis certain nothing can be more unworthy of so august a body as the parliament of Great Britain, than the present place of their assembly: it must be undoubtedly a great surprize to a foreigner, to be forc'd to enquire for the Parliament House even at the doors; and when he found it, to see it so detach'd in parcels, so incumber'd with wretched apartments, and so contemptible in the whole."*

Great Parliamentarians of the 18th and 19th centuries

Edmund Burke
"Your representative owes you, not his industry only, but his judgment; and he betrays instead of serving you if he sacrifices it to your opinion."
Speech to the Electors of Bristol (1774)

William Pitt the Elder
"There are many things a parliament cannot do. It cannot make itself executive, nor dispose of offices which belong to the crown. It cannot take any man's property, even that of the meanest cottager, as in the case of enclosures, without his being heard."
Speech in the House of Commons (1766)

Benjamin Disraeli
"I am a party man. I believe that, without party, Parliamentary government is impossible. I look upon Parliamentary government as the noblest government in the world, and certainly the one most suited to England."
Speech in Manchester (1872).

"I repeat that all power is a trust; that we are accountable for its exercise; that from the people, and for the people all springs, and all must exist."
Vivian Grey (1826)

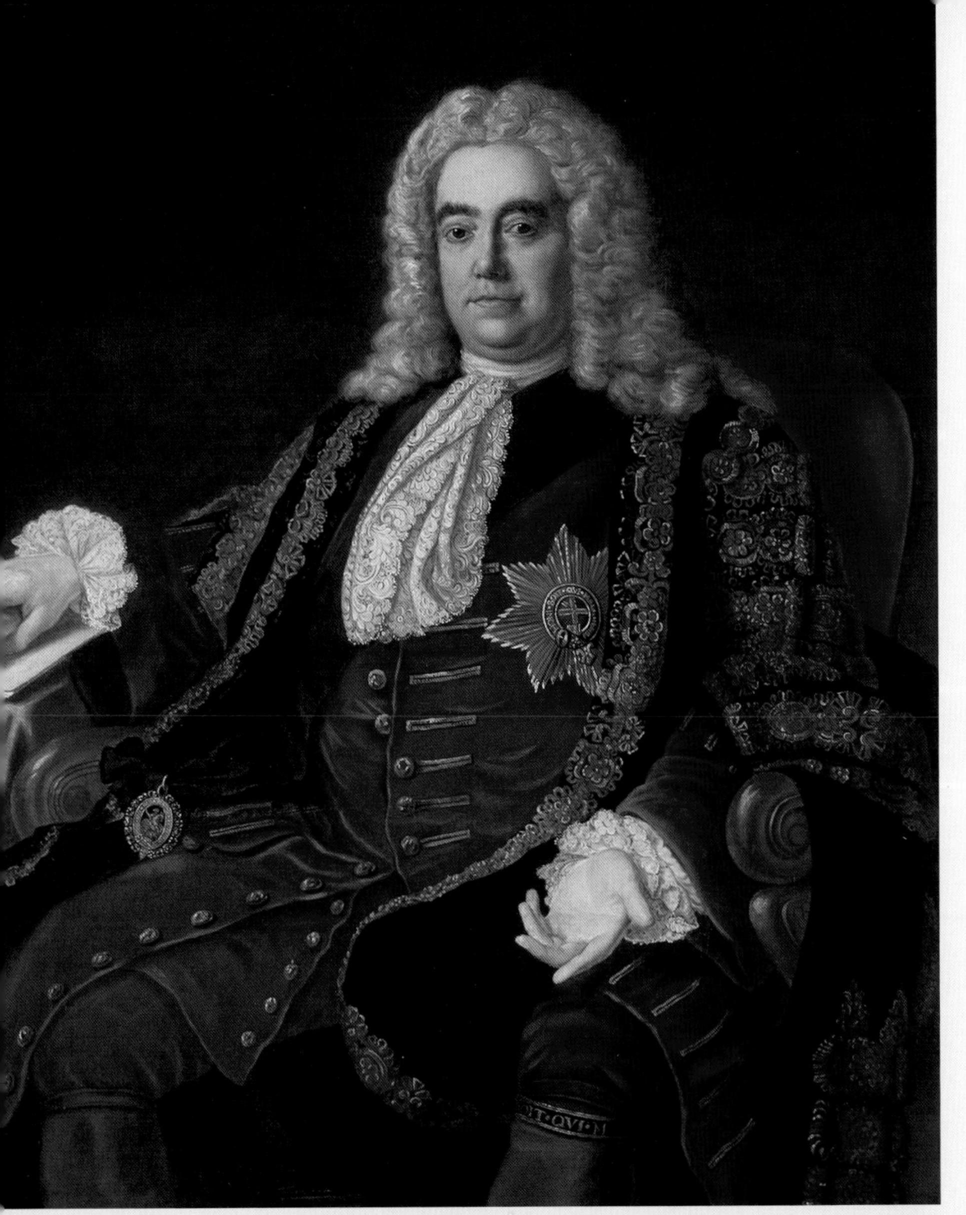

The Prime Minister and the Cabinet

Sir Robert Walpole (1676–1745), whose statue is in St Stephen's Hall, is generally regarded as the first British Prime Minister. Walpole became First Lord of the Treasury – the most senior minister in the government department responsible for finance and the economy. The title 'Prime Minister' was not officially recognised in law until the Ministers of the Crown Act 1937. King George II (1683-1760) presented Walpole with a house at 10 Downing Street in 1732 and it has been the Prime Minister's official residence ever since.

Today, the Prime Minister is the head of the Government, and appoints ministers to run departments such as HM Treasury, the Home Office, the Foreign and Commonwealth Office and the Ministry of Defence. The Prime Minister chairs the Cabinet, which is made up of the leading ministers – usually called Secretaries of State – in each department.

Sir Robert Walpole, 1st Earl of Orford
Stephen Slaughter, oil on canvas, 1742 [WOA 2748]

Walpole, wearing his robes of Chancellor of the Exchequer, is painted in the final year of his premiership.

The assassination of Spencer Perceval

At 5.15 in the afternoon of 11 May 1812, Prime Minister Spencer Perceval (b. 1762) was fatally shot as he entered the House of Commons lobby. The assassin was John Bellingham (1770-1812), a merchant who felt he was owed compensation by the British Government for being wrongly imprisoned in Russia. He was hanged for murder the following week.

Death of Spencer Perceval
Unknown artist, print [WOA 5825]

Tally sticks, *c.* 1293-1294, similar to those burnt in 1834.

Parliamentary Archives, HL/PO/RO/1/195

THE GREAT FIRE OF 1834 AND THE NEW PALACE

A great fire took place on the night of 16 October 1834 when two workmen in the House of Lords disposed of a large number of Exchequer tally sticks – notched pieces of wood used in tax collection – by burning them in the furnaces under the House of Lords Chamber. The panelling above caught fire, and the resulting blaze destroyed most of the Palace of Westminster. Fortunately, Westminster Hall was saved, as were parts of the 1520s cloisters and the lower level of St Stephen's Chapel, now the Chapel of St Mary Undercroft.

The Palace of Westminster was rebuilt after the fire to designs by the architect Charles Barry. The new building was Parliament's first purpose-built home and contained greatly improved facilities. The House of Lords occupied its new Chamber from 1847 and the Commons Chamber was ready in 1852. Libraries for the two Houses were created in the early 19th century, and dining rooms replaced previously chaotic catering arrangements. The rebuilding was completed by 1870.

The law courts that had for so long been a feature of Westminster Hall and its surroundings were removed when new Courts of Justice in the Strand were completed in 1882. An annexe with a Grand Committee Room was completed in the north-west corner of Westminster Hall by 1888. It has been used since 1999 as an additional debating Chamber by the House of Commons.

The Destruction of the Houses of Lords and Commons by Fire on 16th October 1834
William Heath, lithograph, 1834 [WOA 589]

The fire spread quickly through the House of Lords. This dramatic view from Abingdon Street captures the scale of the task facing the fire fighters.

Fire 1834: View from Lambeth Shore of the Palace of Westminster
David Hall McKewan
Watercolour, 1834
[WOA 54]

The fire raged all night. It was a spectacle that drew large crowds, many gathering in boats on the Thames.

Panoramic View of the Ruins of the Late Houses of Parliament
George Scharf senior
Oil on paper, 1835
[WOA 3793]

In a scene of devastation the morning after the fire, the burned-out building on the right is all that remains of the Commons Chamber. The three empty windows are an eerie reminder of centuries of debate.

Westminster
Henry Pether
Oil on canvas,
c. 1857–58 [WOA 7115]

By 1858 the Palace of Westminster was in the final phase of construction, with work on the uppermost part of the Victoria Tower and the faces of the Clock Tower still going on. Red-sailed sloops continued to deliver supplies of stone. Within only a few years of this painting Westminster Bridge was rebuilt and the monumental stone walls of the embankment built, which reduced the width of the Thames.

Getting the vote

Universal suffrage – the right for all adults to vote – has existed in the United Kingdom since 1928. Before that, certain groups of people were not allowed to vote. Catholics, for example, were barred from voting until the Catholic Emancipation Act 1829.

Before 1832, only a small number of men who met strict criteria were entitled to vote and no women could vote at all.

During the 19th century, the vote was gradually extended to about 60% of adult men. The first organised campaigns for votes for women began in the 1860s. The movement gathered pace from 1897 onwards with the foundation of the National Union of Women's Suffrage Societies under Millicent Fawcett. In 1918, the Representation of the People Act gave the vote to all men over the age of 21, and to women over the age of 30 who met certain criteria. The Equal Franchise Act 1928 finally extended the vote to women on equal terms with men. The voting age was lowered in 1969 to 18.

PARLIAMENT AND PUBLIC IN THE 19TH CENTURY

From the late 18th century, there was a major increase in public demand to participate in politics. Thousands of people signed petitions calling for the abolition of the slave trade and slavery and also for the reform of Parliament. Big public demonstrations took place in 1839, 1842 and 1848 as a result of the Chartist campaign for political reform. The Great Reform Act of 1832, with further legislation in 1867 and 1884, gradually extended the right to vote among men. The 19th century saw the start of the campaign for women's suffrage. Women were finally granted the right to vote in 1918 and the right to vote on the same terms as men in 1928.

Parliamentary reporting had long been important in the increasing number of newspapers, and the two Houses for the first time provided space for reporters. The Official Report of proceedings – known as *Hansard* – was formally established in 1909 and the reporters still occupy prime positions in the two Chambers. In the Lords they sit in a raised position in one corner of the floor of the Chamber, and in the Commons they have two seats in the centre of the Gallery above the Speaker's Chair, immediately above the clock.

An Act to amend the Representation of the People in England and Wales (the 'Great Reform Act'), 2&3 William IV, c. 45, 1832.

Parliamentary Archives, HL/PO/PU/1/1832/2&3W4N147

Nancy Langhorne, Viscountess Astor
Zsigmond Kisfaludi Strobl
Plaster, 1933 [WOA S221]

Richard Coeur de Lion
Baron Carlo Marochetti
Bronze, 1856 [WOA S74]

The south end of Westminster Hall after bombing in 1940 with the equestrian statue of Richard I. The sword was damaged by shrapnel. Bent but not broken, it became a symbol of Britain's wartime resilience.

Suffragette demonstration in the Ladies Gallery, House of Commons, on 28 October 1908. A campaigner from the Women's Freedom League chained herself to a grille covering the gallery window. The grille had to be removed to allow her to be freed.

House of Commons Library, *Illustrated London News*, 7 November 1908

A place of unrest

The Palace of Westminster was occasionally a place of violence, not least during the anti-Catholic Gordon riots in 1780, when demonstrators nearly managed to enter both Houses.

In 1812, the Prime Minister, Spencer Perceval, was shot dead in the lobby of the Commons.

In 1885, supporters of the Fenian movement, which was fighting for Irish independence, placed bombs in the Commons Chamber and Chapel of St Mary Undercroft.

During the Second World War, the House of Lords was struck by a bomb which went straight through the floor of the Chamber without exploding. The House of Commons was destroyed by bombing on the night of 10 May 1941 and subsequently rebuilt by the architect Giles Gilbert Scott (see page 55).

Women in Parliament

Viscountess Rhondda (1883-1958), pictured right, was a hereditary woman peer, who was denied the opportunity to sit in the House of Lords following a famous test case before the Lords Committee for Privileges in 1922. She was an active suffragette in her youth, a leading feminist between the wars, a magazine proprietor and a successful businesswoman. She lived to see the passage of the Life Peerages Act 1958, which enabled women to sit in the Lords, but died before the first four women life peers took their seats that October. In the Commons, the first woman MP to be elected was Constance Markievicz, née Gore-Booth (1868-1927), a Sinn Fein activist elected for Dublin St. Patrick's in 1918. She, like all Sinn Fein members, never took her seat at Westminster. The first woman MP to take her seat was Nancy, Viscountess Astor (1879-1964), pictured left, elected for Plymouth Sutton in 1919.

Margaret Haig Thomas, Viscountess Rhondda
Alice Mary Burton, oil on canvas, 1931 [WOA 7177]

Suffragettes in Parliament

Women who campaigned for the right to vote using peaceful means, such as petitioning and lobbying, were known as 'suffragists'. From the early 20th century some women adopted more militant and often illegal tactics such as attacks on property, and they came to be known as 'suffragettes' after the term was used in a newspaper article in 1906. They campaigned tirelessly to be allowed to vote, and a number of reminders of their activity can be found in Parliament.

On 2 April 1911, the night of the census, a suffragette named Emily Wilding Davison (1872-1913) hid overnight in a cupboard in the Chapel of St Mary Undercroft. She wanted to ensure that her address on the night of the census was recorded as the House of Commons to emphasise her claim to political equality with men. She died two years later from injuries she received following a protest at the Epsom Derby, when she ran on to the racecourse in front of the King's horse. A commemorative plaque was installed in the cupboard by Tony Benn MP (b. 1925).

Dadabhai Naoroji
V R Rao
Oil on canvas, *c.* 1906
[WOA 1539]

Dadabhai Naoroji was Liberal MP for Finsbury Central from 1892 to 1895 and was one of at least three 19th century MPs of Indian origin. The others were Mancherjee Bhownaggree, who represented Bethnal Green North-East (1895-1905) and Shapurji Saklatvala, the Labour (later Communist) MP for Battersea North (1922-9). Learie Constantine, a cricketer, lawyer and campaigner against race discrimination originally from Trinidad, became the first recorded black Member of the House of Lords when he was made a life peer in 1969. David Thomas Pitt, an esteemed general practitioner, champion of migrant communities and campaigner against race discrimination, became the second in 1975. Today, about one in 20 of the Members of each House has a minority ethnic background.

The House of Lords, 1961-2
Alfred Reginald Thomson
Oil on canvas, 1964
[WOA 1704]

20TH CENTURY REFORMS

The 20th century saw significant changes in the relationship between the House of Commons and House of Lords. The House of Lords' rejection of the Liberal Government's 1909 budget caused a political crisis while the House of Commons struggled to assert its democratic mandate. This culminated in the Parliament Act of 1911 which removed the House of Lords' ability to veto legislation on taxation and spending, and only allowed it to delay other Acts. In 1949, the maximum period of delay was reduced from two years to one.

Membership of the House of Lords also evolved. At the start of the century, most of its Members were hereditary peers: their right to sit and vote came from the title they had inherited and passed on to their descendants.

In 1958, the Life Peerages Act allowed people to be made Members of the House of Lords for life only. The House of Lords has, as a result, become more diverse in its membership, and an increasingly active Chamber. Further changes took place in 1999, when all but 92 hereditary peers were excluded, and in 2009, when the Law Lords left to form the newly-created Supreme Court, which occupies a building opposite the Palace on the other side of Parliament Square.

One way in which the Commons' work changed in the 20th century was with the introduction in 1979 of a new system of select committees to scrutinise the work of government departments. This enormously enhanced MPs' ability to hold the Government to account, and improved public understanding of Parliament's role. The Lords' investigative committee work expanded when the United Kingdom joined the European Union and it developed a committee system to scrutinise EU policies affecting many aspects of national life. Both Houses' select committee oral evidence sessions are open to the public and are webcast on the internet.

Hansard is the official report of all the speeches made in the two Houses' Chambers and Committees. Accounts of parliamentary debates appeared in newspapers from the 18th century, and various publishers experimented with printing compiled reports. In 1812, Thomas Curson Hansard (1776–1833), the son of the Commons printer Luke Hansard (1752-1828), took over a series called *The Parliamentary Debates* from William Cobbett (1763-1835), which became known as 'Hansard'. Charles Dickens (1812-70) worked for a time as a parliamentary reporter. In 1909, Hansard reporters became employees of each House. *Hansard* is prepared every day the Houses sit, and speeches can be read on the website *www.parliament.uk* as soon as they are ready.

Luke Hansard
by unknown artist
after original by
Samuel Lane,
Oil on canvas [WOA 1500]

The Other Picture: A View of the Smoking Room and Library of the House of Commons in
for the House by One hundred and fifty six of the Members of Parliament who were not i

The House of Lords experimented with televising its proceedings in 1985, and the Commons followed suit in 1989. Today, BBC Parliament broadcasts live coverage of the House of Commons, as well as business in the House of Lords. Moments of great political theatre, such as the weekly half-hour Prime Minister's Questions, now regularly feature on news bulletins, and live broadcasts are often made from places in and around the Palace of Westminster, including Central Lobby.

Today, Parliament is as open as possible. It has developed an extensive website, all its public proceedings are webcast, and the public can attend parliamentary debates or hearings and take guided tours.

The Other Picture
Andrew Festing
Oil on canvas, 1988
[WOA 3373]

In 1987, 156 Backbench MPs who had not been included in the official 1986 House of Commons painting (see pages 58-59) commissioned their own painting. Members were grouped together in rooms they frequently used, such as the Smoking Room and the House of Commons Library.

The Last Judgments of the Law Lords
Sergei Pavlenko
Oil on canvas, 2009
[WOA 7122]

At the end of July 2009 the Law Lords sat in the Lords Chamber to give judgments for the last time before moving to the new Supreme Court. It was a fundamental change to the role of the House of Lords.

Committee Room 14, also known as the Gladstone Room, has a series of paintings showing 19th century Parliamentarians who served during Gladstone's (1809-98) four terms as Prime Minister.

The parliamentary oath is a religious oath of loyalty to the crown. In the past, it had to be taken on the Bible, which effectively prevented non-Christians and people of no faith from taking up their seats. Furthermore, Roman Catholics were unable to take their seats until the Catholic Emancipation Act was passed in 1829, allowing Daniel O'Connell (1775-1847) to take his seat as the Member for County Clare in Ireland to which he had been elected the previous year. The first practising Jew to enter Parliament was Lionel Rothschild (1808-79), who was elected in 1847 but was refused permission to take his seat until 1858. Charles Bradlaugh (1833-91), an avowed atheist, was elected in 1880 and campaigned tirelessly so that he could 'affirm' loyalty rather than swearing a religious oath. He finally secured this right for himself and subsequent MPs in the Oaths Act of 1888.

Backbench MPs sit on benches behind the front benches, which are mainly reserved for Ministers on the Government side and shadow Ministers on the Opposition side. The same applies in the Lords. The Backbench Business Committee gives Backbench MPs the opportunity to hold debates on subjects of their choice. It is considered the particular duty of the Speaker to stand up for the rights of Backbench MPs.

Prime Minister's Questions: The Prime Minister comes to the Chamber of the House of Commons every Wednesday at 12 noon when Parliament is in session to answer questions from MPs, including the Leader of the Opposition. The Chamber and public galleries are always packed for the event, which can be a noisy, theatrical occasion. Microphones hanging from the ceiling pick up the questions and answers for broadcast, and concealed speakers in the benches enable the MPs in the Chamber to hear what is said above the background noise.

Committee Room 14 (pictured left) has witnessed many stormy private meetings. The 1922 Committee, which is in effect the organisation of Conservative Backbenchers, and the Parliamentary Labour Party, which is made up of Labour MPs, hold their weekly meetings here.

Committee Room 14 is larger than most of the rooms used for public Committee sittings on Bills or specific topics but is set out in the same way, with the Chair seated at the table on the dais at one end of the room and the Members sitting on facing benches down each side. It has been used mainly for parliamentary Committees with a large number of members, such as the Welsh Grand Committee comprising all Members sitting for Welsh constituencies. Committee Rooms are open to the public when they are being used for legislative and similar meetings, or for public select committee hearings.

Tour

The Palace of Westminster contains some of the finest art and craftsmanship that the nation has produced. This chapter looks at those parts of the building on the tour, and at the treasures they contain, many of which were specially commissioned for the building.

Most of the Palace's decoration was designed when it was rebuilt after the fire in 1834 in the reign of Queen Victoria (1819-1901). Her husband, Prince Albert (1819-61), chaired the Fine Arts Commission established in 1841 to mastermind the project. The Commission's vision was to combine fine art and sculpture with the building's architecture. The scale of the challenge was considerable; for example, over 100 wall compartments had to be filled with paintings and the Commission's 20-year undertaking was an important period for state patronage of the arts in Britain.

Historical themes were chosen for the decoration. Beginning with Saxon times, the paintings and statues form a rich pageant of national history, combining Victorian morality and educational values. The struggles of the Civil War are depicted, as is the Glorious Revolution. The largest paintings commissioned cover much of the walls on either side of the Royal Gallery and depict Napoleon's defeats in the battles of Trafalgar and Waterloo. Over life-sized marble statues of parliamentarians line St Stephen's Hall, bringing alive those whose voices echoed there in previous centuries when it was the site of the House of Commons Chamber.

The Fine Arts Commission held exhibitions in Westminster Hall to attract the best artists and sculptors. William Dyce (1806-64), Daniel Maclise (1806-70) and Charles West Cope (1811-90) were among the small group of artists selected. However, the choice of fresco, considered the most noble form of art for wall paintings but also the most technically difficult, together with the ambitious scale of the project, meant that some of the Commission's schemes were never finished.

The paintings and sculpture from the Victorian age form the nucleus of the Parliamentary Art Collection. Successive generations have added works of art, ensuring that this unique national collection continues to document the work of Parliament, past and present.

The House of Lords, 1851
Joseph Nash, gouache [WOA 2939]

Queen Victoria sits on the Throne, with Prince Albert on her left, at the State Opening of Parliament on 4 February 1851. In the foreground is Speaker Shaw-Lefevre and to the right Palmerston, Lord John Russell and Disraeli.

The frescoes above the throne have been completed, but the Magna Carta statues have yet to be added to the niches between the stained glass windows. Ladies are seated on the benches: it became fashionable in the 19th century for Members' female guests to take the peers' place at the State Opening.

Norman Porch

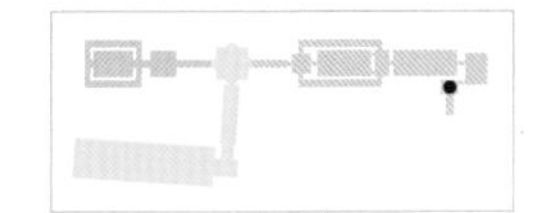

On the day of the State Opening of Parliament, the monarch arrives in a state coach under the arch of the Victoria Tower and goes up the 26 steps of the Royal Staircase to the Norman Porch. It is called the Norman Porch because it was intended to house statues of Norman kings at the start of a procession of royal statues running through the building. The statues were never commissioned and in the 1960s a display of busts of Prime Ministers who were Members of the House of Lords was installed.

Edward Barry (1830-80), Charles Barry's son, completed the Norman Porch. He added the mosaic decoration to the ceiling and a floor made of British and Irish limestones polished to resemble marble. The room's two stained glass windows were designed by Pugin. They show Edward the Confessor, who built the original royal palace, and a young Queen Victoria, during whose reign the new Palace was built.

Two wall compartments were designed for fresco paintings of Canute and Elizabeth I but now contain portraits of Queen Victoria seated on the chair of state used by the monarch at the State Opening, and Edward, 1st Baron Thurlow, who was Lord Chancellor between 1778 and 1792.

Interior of the richly decorated Norman Porch, with marble busts of Prime Ministers, seen from the top of the Royal Staircase.

The stone vaulting was given a glistening gold and coloured mosaic decoration by Charles Barry's son, Edward, who completed the Palace when his father died in 1860. The patterns depict the Tudor rose; carved angels bear shields of England, Ireland, Scotland and Wales. The mosaics were made by Italian craftsmen working for the firm Salviati in Venice.

The stained glass windows depict Edward the Confessor (pictured) and Queen Victoria, the two monarchs most closely associated with the Palace of Westminster.

The crowned portcullis is the emblem of both Houses of Parliament and is a recurring decorative feature throughout the building. It is found on curtains, wallpaper, furniture, and carved into the stone and wood of the building. It is even cast into the metal of Big Ben, the great bell in the Clock Tower.

The portcullis symbolises strength and security as it was a defensive gate used in many medieval castles; the addition of a crown makes it a royal symbol, which the monarch grants Parliament a licence to use.

Both Henry VII and Henry VIII used it as their badge because it was a symbol of the Beaufort family of Henry VII's mother, Lady Margaret. The symbol, together with the Tudor rose and fleur de lys, was used to decorate Henry VII's chapel in Westminster Abbey, and was copied when the Palace of Westminster was rebuilt after a fire in 1834.

Portcullis Sculpture
LPB Sculpture and Design, bronze, 1991 [WOA S230]

Queen's Robing Room

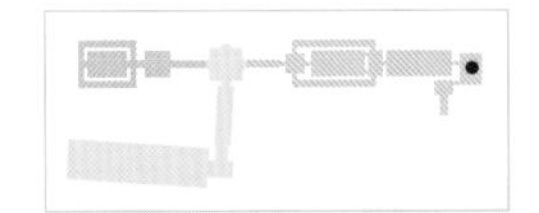

The Queen's Robing Room is where, before the State Opening of Parliament, the monarch puts on the Imperial State Crown and parliamentary robes.

The decoration of the room was completed by Edward Barry. Its theme is the legend of King Arthur, which the Victorians felt illustrated the power, privileges, virtues and duties invested in the monarch; 18 carved oak relief panels depict scenes from the legend. Above, frescoes show five of seven chivalric virtues: Courtesy, Religion, Generosity, Mercy and Hospitality. Fidelity and Courage are missing because the artist, William Dyce, died before completing the series. Portraits of Queen Victoria and Prince Albert stand in their place on either side of the chair of state.

The ceiling ribs form a complex geometric pattern. The panels between them are decorated with symbols of royalty and Parliament, such as the portcullis, as is the wooden parquet floor. The 'grisaille' glass in the windows was designed by John Hardman Powell. The fireplace makes further references to royalty, especially Queen Victoria, with crowns and other emblems, and is flanked by the figures of St George and St Michael. One wall panel conceals a hidden door leading to a small washroom, while another has a door to the adjoining Prince Consort's Robing Room, which is now used as Peers' offices.

Following the bombing of the House of Commons in the Second World War, the House of Lords sat in the Robing Room between June 1941 and October 1950, and the House of Commons used the Lords Chamber.

The Robing Room is richly decorated with royal symbols and motifs. The fireplace is made from British marbles. Coats of arms below the ceiling represent the Knights of the Round Table. Above the two doors are carved and decorated coats of arms of England, Ireland and Scotland. Opposite the fireplace is a single throne which was made for Queen Victoria after the death of her husband.

The wooden ceiling was designed in 16th century style. The centre of each panel has the 'VR' motif for *Victoria Regina (Queen Victoria)*, with other royal symbols surrounding it. J G Crace applied the painted decoration and gilding.

Queen Victoria
after original by Franz Xaver Winterhalter
Oil on canvas, c. 1859 [WOA 3154]

Prince Albert
after original by Franz Xaver Winterhalter
Oil on canvas, c. 1859 [WOA 3155]

RELIGION

Royal Gallery

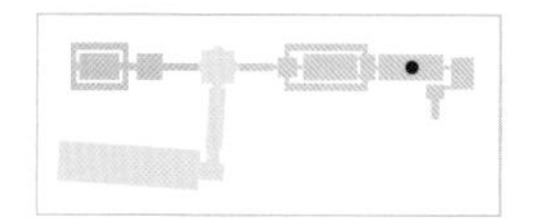

Originally called the Victoria Gallery, this is the largest room in the Palace of Westminster and is designed to be imposing. It forms the main part of the processional route for the State Opening of Parliament. Guests watch the royal party leave the Robing Room and process along its 110ft (33.5m) length towards the Lords Chamber from specially installed seating. Barry and Pugin ornamented almost all the elements of this huge space, including the ceiling, wallpaper, wood panelling and vast expanse of tiles, sections of which are surrounded by Latin inscriptions in intricate gothic lettering: *Domine Salvam Fac Reginam Nostram (God Save Our Queen)* and *Cor Reginae in Manu Domini (the heart of the Queen is in the hand of the Lord).*

The Fine Arts Commission intended to fill the room's 18 wall compartments with paintings showing 'the military history and glory of the country'. Subjects ranging from Boadicea to Waterloo were selected. However, only two paintings were undertaken, both depicting British victories in the Napoleonic wars: the Battle of Trafalgar ended the threat of a French invasion, and the Battle of Waterloo marked Napoleon's final defeat. Waterloo was started by Daniel Maclise in fresco, but technical difficulties led Prince Albert to suggest using the German technique of waterglass (liquid silica was sprayed over the completed painting to bond the pigments permanently to the plaster wall). Prince Albert also helped Maclise to research uniforms, providing him with sketches (see below). On its completion, Waterloo was described in the press as the "greatest work of its class that has ever been seen in England". The other 16 compartments today contain portraits of monarchs and their consorts from George I to Elizabeth II. Many are copies of paintings in the Royal Collection. Building on the military theme, the sculptor John Birnie Philip (1824–75) was commissioned in 1867 to produce eight statues of kings and queens who reigned at the time of great wars in English history.

The House of Lords sat in the Royal Gallery in 1980 while repairs were carried out to the roof of its Chamber. Members of the House of Lords now use this room as an informal working area, but it is also employed for state occasions such as addresses to both Houses of Parliament by foreign dignitaries – including Emperor Haile Selassie of Ethiopia in 1954, Chancellor Willy Brandt of West Germany in 1970, U.S. President Bill Clinton in 1995 and former UN Secretary-General Kofi Annan in 2007 – and for temporary exhibitions. Display cases contain records from the Parliamentary Archives which change several times a year.

Marshal Blucher wearing a forage cap
Prince Albert, pencil sketch [WOA 4496]

Prince Albert was a great source of support for Daniel Maclise while he researched and painted the 'Waterloo' mural. It is remarkable that Albert made time to prepare sketches such as this.

Interior of the 110ft (33.5m) long Royal Gallery, looking north towards the Prince's Chamber. Full length royal portraits hang on two levels around the walls against the rich backdrop of gilded and painted decoration.

'Trafalgar' in 1805 and 'Waterloo' in 1815 were both battles which had taken place within living memory when the Palace of Westminster was being built in the mid 19th century. As part of his research Maclise talked to soldiers and sailors who had taken part and their accounts give these paintings particular poignancy and realism.

The paintings were the largest works commissioned for the building. Together they document the final defeat of Napoleon's naval and land forces, each illustrating the moment when the battle had been fought and won and victory was assured.

The battles themselves were of great national significance. The Battle of Trafalgar ended the threat of a French invasion of Britain, and made Admiral Lord Nelson a national hero. The Battle of Waterloo marked Napoleon's final defeat, bringing to an end more than 20 years of war in Europe, and sealed the Duke of Wellington's reputation as a great military commander.

The Death of Nelson
Daniel Maclise, waterglass, 1865 [WOA 3247]

Admiral Nelson's flagship the Victory is shown locked in battle with the French ship the *Redoutable*. Nelson, shot through the shoulder, is close to death as he surveys the scene of battle, but knows that victory is assured. The painting shows heroism on a grand scale, with the power of the action convincingly expressed.

The Meeting of Wellington and Blucher after Waterloo
Daniel Maclise, Waterglass, 1859 [WOA 3246]

To the Victorian audience the meeting of Marshal Blucher, the leader of the Prussian forces, with the Duke of Wellington after the Battle of Waterloo symbolised the Anglo-Prussian Alliance. Wellington's face shows a mixture of emotions, calm resolution mingled with sadness, at the loss of life of his gallant soldiers; there is triumph in the face of Blucher.

Ld DARNLEY
A BOLEYN
K HOWARD

Prince's Chamber

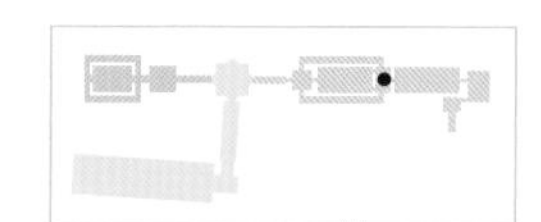

The Prince's Chamber serves as an ante-room to the House of Lords. It inherited its name from the room next to the Queen's Chamber in the medieval Palace, which was used by the monarch's eldest son, the Prince of Wales. It is where a ceremonial search of the Palace cellars and basements starts on the morning of the State Opening of Parliament since the Gunpowder plot in 1605 (see page 7). When the House is sitting, peers collect messages left for them here and meet at the octagonal tables which Pugin specially designed to accommodate small conferences.

The Fine Arts Commission decided on a Tudor theme for the room. Twelve bronze reliefs around the walls depict scenes from Tudor history below 28 portraits of Tudor royalty and their contemporaries. The portraits are designed to evoke the style of the Tudor period but were painted centuries later in the 1850s by students from the Royal College of Art with their tutor Richard Burchett. They are made to look as though they were painted on gilded leather but are actually oil paint on timber panels. A series of paintings of the Spanish Armada of 1588 looks down on the room from high level. These are based on tapestries that hung in the House of Lords until they were destroyed in the 1834 fire. Richard Burchett painted one – *The English Fleet Pursuing the Spanish Fleet against Fowey* – in the 1850s, which is directly above the statue of Queen Victoria. The series was completed in 2010 when the final five pictures were painted and the whole set installed.

The chamber is also home to John Gibson's (1750-1866) monumental statue of Queen Victoria, enthroned with a sceptre in her left hand and a crown of laurel in her right. The images carved on the pedestal show at the front Commerce, a female figure with a ship, anchor and merchandise; on the left is Science, a young man with geometric symbols and instruments; on the right is Industry (or the Useful Arts) with telegraph wires and a steam engine in the background. The central statue is flanked by the figures of Justice and Clemency.

King Henry VIII
Richard Burchett, oil on panel, 1854-60 [WOA 3190]

Drake takes De Valdes's Galleon; the Lord Admiral Pursues the Enemy (detail)
Anthony Oakshett, oil on canvas, 2010 [WOA 7124]

The defeat of the Armada was England's most notable military achievement in the Elizabethan age and removed the threat of a Spanish invasion. This is the third in a series of six paintings showing the engagements between the English and Spanish fleets in the summer of 1588. In 2007 Mark Pigott OBE generously donated funds to the House of Lords to enable this historic set of paintings to be created.

State Opening of Parliament

The State Opening is the highlight of the parliamentary year, when the monarch comes to the Palace of Westminster to open Parliament's new session.

SIGNIFICANCE

The State Opening is an important royal ceremony. The occasion is also constitutionally significant because it assembles the monarch and Members of both the Lords and the Commons, who together formally govern the country. It is a major political event, because the monarch reads a speech which outlines the Government's legislative plans.

TRADITION

The ancient tradition of the State Opening goes back at least to the reign of Henry VIII, who is known to have opened Parliament in person. Guy Fawkes and his co-conspirators planned to use the State Opening to assassinate James I on 5 November 1605 by blowing up the Lords Chamber with gunpowder. A ceremonial search of the Palace's basements and cellars still takes place on the morning of the event.

Queen Victoria established the modern pattern for the State Opening when she opened Parliament for the first time in the new Palace of Westminster in 1852. Since the early 20th century, the monarch has nearly always attended the State Opening.

THE CEREMONY

With a military escort, the monarch travels in a state coach down the Mall, across Horse Guards Parade and along Whitehall to the Palace of Westminster. On arrival at the Sovereign's Entrance at the base of the Victoria Tower, the Royal Standard is raised and gun salutes are fired by the King's Troop regiment in Hyde Park and the Tower of London.

The monarch is met by the Earl Marshal and Lord Great Chamberlain at the Sovereign's Entrance, ascends the Royal Staircase and walks through the Norman Porch to the Robing Room to put on the Imperial State Crown and parliamentary robes.

The monarch then follows a processional route through the Royal Gallery, which is packed with over 600 guests, to the House of Lords Chamber. The Royal Procession is led by senior parliamentary and government officers, including the Lord Chancellor and Lord Speaker. The Great Sword of State and the Cap of Maintenance, symbols of sovereign power and authority, are carried in front of the monarch.

The Lords Chamber is full of bishops, peers, judges and guests including foreign ambassadors and other dignitaries. Many wear national or ceremonial dress. Black Rod is sent to summon Members of the House of Commons. The door to the Commons Chamber is shut in his face. This practice dates back to the Civil War and symbolises the Commons' autonomy from the monarchy. Black Rod must strike the door three times to gain admission.

MPs then process to the Lords. The procession is led by the Serjeant at Arms, carrying the House of Commons Mace, followed by the Speaker and Black Rod. In the Lords

The Queen accompanied by the Duke of Edinburgh in procession to the Lords Chamber. The monarch's bodyguard line the route. The building of the Royal Gallery in the 19th century allowed members of the public to see the monarch wearing the crown at the State Opening for the first time.

Yeomen of the Guard wear their scarlet embroidered state dress which dates from Tudor times. Armed with swords and carrying lanterns, they prepare to start the ceremonial search of the Palace vaults before the State Opening begins.

The House of Lords, 1857
Joseph Nash, gouache, 1858 [WOA 2941]

The State Opening of Parliament in December 1857, with Queen Victoria on the throne and Prince Albert on her left, awaiting the arrival of the House of Commons.

The Heralds of the College of Arms attend the monarch at the State Opening.

Black Rod waits in Central Lobby for the signal to summon MPs to listen to the Queen's speech.

Chamber, they position themselves at the entrance to listen to the speech. The Lord Chancellor hands the speech to the monarch who then reads it out from the Throne.

The speech is written by Ministers and reflects the policies of the Government rather than the monarch's personal opinions, because the monarch must remain above party politics. The speech lists the Bills (draft laws) that the Government intends to introduce and is debated in both Houses, each of which approves a formal address to thank the monarch. The final words, 'Other measures will be laid before you', are included so that the Government may also introduce other Bills.

A **'parliament'** runs from one general election to the next (five years). It is broken up into sessions which run for about a year – the 'parliamentary year'. The State Opening takes place on the first day of a new session. The Queen's Speech is the formal start to the year. Neither House can conduct any business until it has been read.

The Queen's Speech, setting out the Government's plans for the next parliamentary session, is delivered to a packed House of Lords Chamber and broadcast to the nation. Extra benches are installed so that as many peers as possible may be seated. Members of the House of Lords wear red robes with a white fur trim and Law Lords wear dark gowns and wigs. Ambassadors and other guests are seated in galleries around the Chamber.

The Queen is seated on the throne with the Duke of Edinburgh to her left and her two Ladies in Waiting standing next to him. Three pageboys stand in the compartment to her right. When the Queen is ready to give the speech, she nods to the Lord Chamberlain, standing to her left. He signals with his staff to Black Rod who goes to summon the MPs to listen to the speech.

Lords Chamber

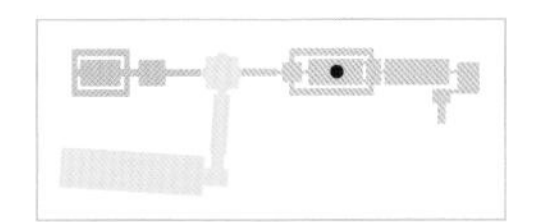

The Lords Chamber was completed in 1847. It was designed to be the grandest room in the Palace as it is the place where three pillars of British society come together: Monarchy, Church, and Parliament. The decoration of this interior was without parallel elsewhere in the Palace of Westminster and exemplifies the successful collaboration between Barry and Pugin.

The Chamber is dominated by the Throne and its surroundings, its gilded ornamentation a reminder that Britain was at the height of its wealth and power when the new Palace was built. At the State Opening of Parliament, the monarch reads the speech seated on the Throne in the centre. At all other times, the Throne is empty, although Privy Counsellors and the eldest child of any serving Member of the House of Lords, amongst others, may sit on its steps to watch the business of the House.

No part of the Chamber is undecorated, except the Woolsack (see right) on which the Lord Speaker sits. It is thought to have been introduced in the 14th century to reflect the economic importance of the wool trade to England. Over the years, its stuffing changed to hair, but in 1938 it was restuffed with wool from England, Scotland, Wales, Northern Ireland and the Commonwealth.

View of the Lords Chamber facing the monarch's throne. Above are paintings showing historical examples of the virtues of religion, chivalry and justice. Paintings on the wall opposite show allegorical examples of the same virtues.

The Throne used by the monarch was designed by Pugin and first used in 1847. Its design is based on the Coronation Chair in Westminster Abbey. It was made by John Webb of Bond Street and is of gilded mahogany decorated with embroidery of the royal coat of arms surrounded by rock crystals.

Crossbench Members in the Lords

Most Members of the House of Lords, like MPs in the Commons, are members of a political party. However, about a quarter are independent. They may signal their separation from party by sitting on the benches which are placed across the Lords Chamber, physically apart from the Government and Opposition benches. These are the Crossbenches and the Members who sit on them are called Crossbenchers.

The Table is in front of the Woolsack in the Lords and the Speaker's Chair in the Commons. It separates the benches for Ministers from those for the Opposition shadow Ministers and bears Despatch Boxes at which Ministers speak. The Table in the House of Lords still bears damage inflicted by Winston Churchill's signet ring during his rousing wartime speeches. Churchill was speaking in the Chamber of the House of Lords because the Commons Chamber was destroyed during the Second World War and MPs sat in the Lords Chamber, while the Lords moved into the Robing Room. This is when the Speaker's Procession first began to go through Central Lobby, in order to reach the Commons' temporary accommodation.

Stained glass windows make up almost half the height of the east and west walls. The designs originally depicted British monarchs but this glass was replaced in the 1950s with heraldic designs after being damaged in the Second World War. The wooden panelling covering the lower part of the east and west walls is the most ornate in the Palace. Above are galleries for peers' guests. The red curtains around the upper railings were introduced to hide ladies' ankles from view as fashions changed and hemlines got higher.

The subjects of the wall paintings, Religion, Justice and Chivalry, were chosen to reflect the 19th century roles of the House of Lords: Lords Spiritual, Law Lords and Lords Temporal. Each subject is illustrated by a pair of paintings: one showing an allegorical representation above the visitors' gallery, and the other showing a historical example above the throne at the opposite end of the room.

Black Rod's full title is the Gentleman Usher of the Black Rod. The office was created in 1350 but the title dates from 1522 and comes from the black ebony staff topped with a golden lion, which is a symbol of the office's authority. Black Rod is appointed by the monarch and is a senior officer of the House of Lords whose duties and responsibilities include security and attending to the monarch in the Lords. Black Rod's ceremonial duties include a role at the State Opening of Parliament when the monarch sends him to summon MPs to listen to the speech (see above and pages 34-35).

The throne canopy (see right) is made of English oak. Its central compartment contains the monarch's throne with the royal coat of arms carved in the wood above and the three lions of England in the surround. Above are the four most important orders of chivalry: St Patrick, the Garter, the Thistle and the Bath, around a central figure of St George. The compartment to the right of the throne has the coat of arms of Queen Victoria's son when he was Prince of Wales: a badge of three ostrich feathers and the German motto *'Ich Dien' (I serve)*. The other compartment has the coat of arms of Queen Victoria's husband. Pugin designed the two 'x-framed' seats usually placed on either side of the Throne. A second throne, which is 1.5 inches (3.8cm) shorter than the monarch's, was made for Queen Alexandra, the wife of Queen Victoria's son, Edward VII, when he acceded to the throne.

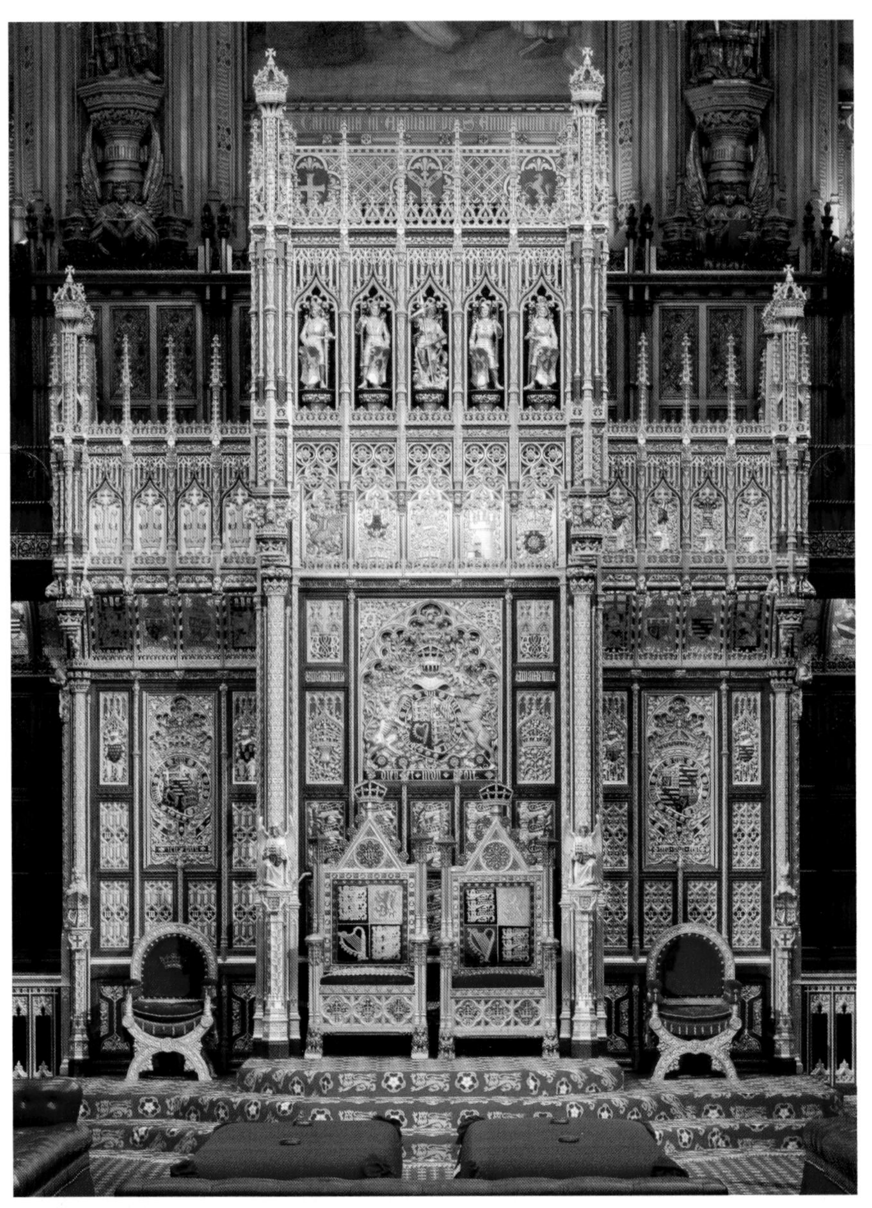

The Lords Chamber facing north towards the Commons and the galleries used by the public and press. Above these are paintings showing allegorical examples of the virtues of religion, chivalry and justice. Paintings on the wall opposite show historical examples of the same virtues.

Eighteen statues of barons and archbishops who sealed the Magna Carta (see page 4) occupy narrow stone niches high in the walls. Fifteen are made of zinc electroplated with copper, a pioneering use of Victorian technology.

Coats of arms, insignia and numerous other references to kings, queens and peerages adorn the Chamber. The ceiling shows ancient emblems (see below), including the white hart (stag) of Richard II (1367-1400), the sun of the House of York, the crown in a bush of Henry VII (1457-1509), the lion passant of England, the lion rampant of Scotland, the harp of Ireland, the rose of England, the pomegranate of Castile, the lily of France and the portcullis of the Beaufort family.

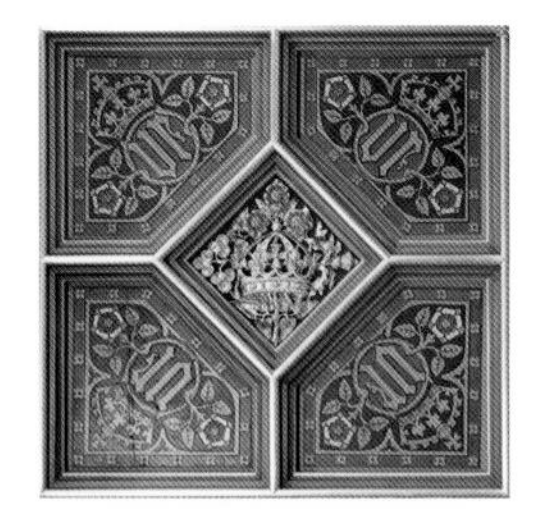

This carved wooden panel is behind the Chair of State belonging to the Prince of Wales. The coat of arms is that of Albert Prince of Wales, later Edward VII; it is surrounded by the chivalric Order of the Garter which had been awarded to him.

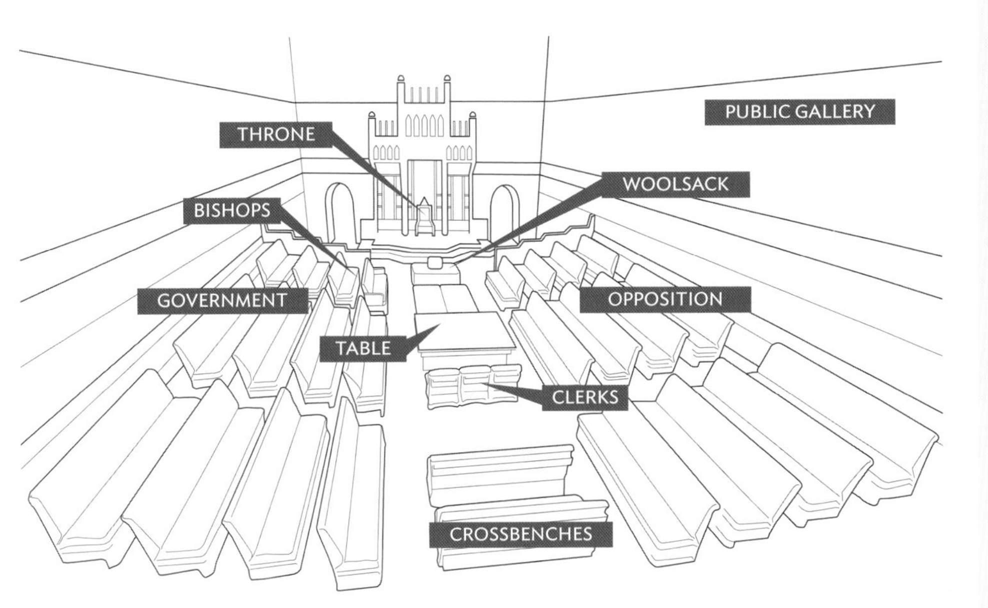

The Lords Chamber seen from the Bar of the House. When the House is sitting, the Lord Speaker sits on the Woolsack, in front of the Mace. Members of the public can watch debates from the mezzanine-level public galleries on either side of the Chamber and above the Bar of the House.

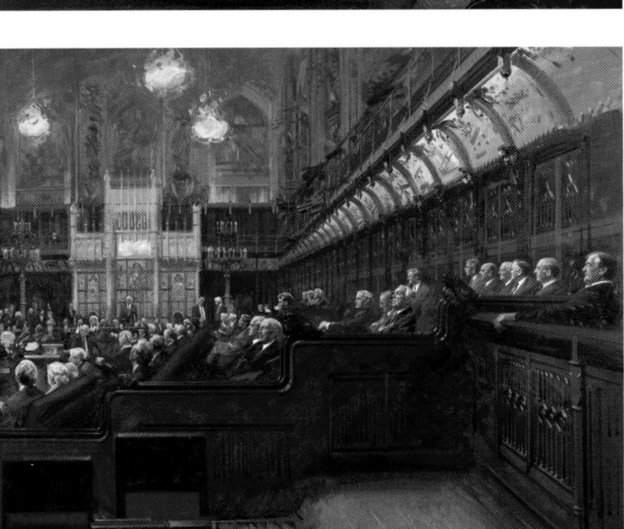

The House of Lords Debating the Queen's Speech, November 1995
Andrew Festing
Oil on canvas, 1998
[WOA 5414]

Each of the six canvases brings to life a different perspective of the debate in the Lords Chamber. Taking the artist over a year to paint, the painting is a virtuoso work, with over 350 individual portraits of peers and officials.

The Lord Speaker is the politically impartial presiding officer in the House of Lords, elected by its Members for up to two five-year terms. The Lord Speaker chairs debates, speaks for the House on ceremonial occasions, and acts as ambassador for its work at home and abroad. Until 2006, a similar role was performed by the Lord Chancellor, but the Constitutional Reform Act 2005 created a separate office. The first Lord Speaker was Baroness Hayman, who served in the role until 2011.

The position of **Lord Chancellor** can be traced back to medieval times and its duties have changed over time. Holders of the post have headed the judiciary and presided over proceedings in the House of Lords, a role now performed by the Lord Speaker. The current Lord Chancellor still performs ceremonial duties at the State Opening of Parliament.

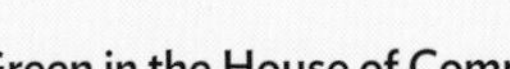

Green in the House of Commons and Red in the House of Lords

The most visible difference between the two Chambers is the colour of the benches on which the MPs and Lords sit. Red is the colour of the Lords because of its associations with royalty, and green the colour of the Commons. The use of green extends back some 300 years, although the origin is uncertain. The colour scheme is reflected in the colour of carpets and upholstery.

Peers Lobby and Peers Corridor

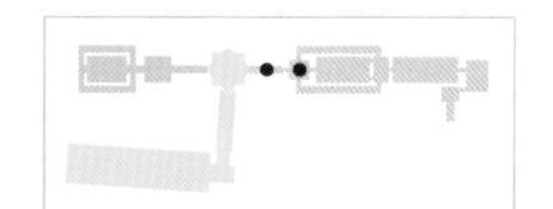

The Peers Lobby is dominated by four heavily moulded arches that lead off to the north, south, east and west. Gold-leafed crowns and foliage surround the Pugin-designed solid brass gates at the entrance to the Chamber to the south. Each gate weighs about three quarters of a tonne. Their design is based on the early 16th century gates to Henry VII's chapel in Westminster Abbey. Members of the House of Lords go through the east and west arches of the lobby to reach the division lobbies for voting which double as corridors. The inscription on the floor tiles *Dieu et mon droit* (from the French for *God and my right*) is the British monarch's motto. It was adopted by Henry V in the 15th century and refers to the monarch's divine right to govern.

The Peers Corridor connects the House of Lords to Central Lobby. It has a series of eight mural paintings by Charles West Cope (1811-90) showing the English Civil War (1642-49), a turbulent period in national history. The battles between Charles I and his royalist supporters, nicknamed Cavaliers, and Parliament, whose supporters were nicknamed Roundheads, reflected a wider struggle for national liberties.

The Peers Corridor facing south from Central Lobby towards the Lords Chamber.

Lord Chancellor John Campbell, 1st Baron Campbell, in Peers' Lobby
R Dudley
Watercolour, 1861
[WOA 2120]

Raking light throws the intricate architectural detail of Peers Lobby into sharp relief, illuminating the bright colours of the painted and gilded decoration and the encaustic tile pavement.

The Embarkation of the Pilgrim Fathers for New England
Charles West Cope
Fresco painting, 1846
[WOA 2892]

Central Lobby

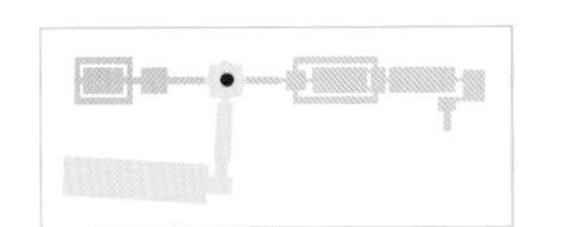

This is the mid-point between the Commons and the Lords, and the main route between the two. Visitors pass through to watch debates in the Chambers, and many people meet and lobby their MPs here. It is often seen in the background on the news as broadcasters are allowed to film here. The west door leads to St Stephen's Hall, and the east to the Lower Waiting Hall and Committee staircase which gives access to the first floor Committee rooms.

Central Lobby is an octagonal space with a decorated stone vault or roof. The intricate shapes between the carved bosses and ribs of the ceiling are filled with mosaics. Statues of kings and queens line each of the eight arches.

Spectators gather in Central Lobby at the heart of the Palace as the Speaker's procession makes its way to the Commons Chamber. The Serjeant at Arms carries the Mace ahead of the Speaker.

Central Lobby facing north with the Commons Chamber in the background. Stone statues of monarchs line the arches and there are marble statues of 19th century politicians (William Gladstone to the left and Sir Stafford Henry Northcote to the right). The tile floor has national flower symbols: the rose for England, thistle for Scotland, shamrock for Ireland, and leek for Wales. As in the Norman Porch, Charles Barry's son, Edward, added the mosaic decoration to the vaulted ceiling.

St David
Edward John Poynter, mosaic, 1898 [WOA 4255]

SAINT
DAVID
FOR
WALES

The Fine Arts Commission established the decorative scheme for the large mosaics in Central Lobby's four arched compartments: *"...bearing in mind that the Hall is the central point of the whole building...the nationality of the component parts of the United Kingdom should be the idea here illustrated"*. The use of mosaics rather than paintings reflects the Victorian Arts and Crafts Movement's success in promoting craft techniques. The mosaics depict the four patron saints of England, Ireland, Scotland and Wales. St George for England and St David for Wales, together with the main ceiling, were completed in the late 19th century. The mosaic work was undertaken by a Venetian firm, Salviati, which also worked on the Albert Memorial in Kensington Gardens. St Andrew for Scotland and St Patrick for Ireland were not undertaken until the 1920s when Robert Anning Bell (1863-1933), of the Royal College of Art, was commissioned to design them. Miss Gertrude Martin, one of the few women to have worked on the arts in the Palace, led the craft team which undertook the work.

A Latin inscription around the central circle of floor tiles is from Psalm 127 and reads *Nisi dominus edificaverit domum in vanum laboraverunt qui edificant eam (Except the Lord build the House, they labour in vain that build it)*. A repeated inscription around the outer edge of the tiles reads *Domine Salvam Fac Reginam Nostram Victoriam (God Save our Queen Victoria)*.

The Tower above Central Lobby is 300ft (91m) high. After the fire of 1834, MPs wanted the new building to be well ventilated. A tower was built above Central Lobby to act as a chimney, drawing stale air out from the building and expelling it through its spire (see left). Unfortunately, the system, designed by David Reid (1805-63), Ventilator to the House of Commons, did not work, and when MPs moved into the new Chamber in 1852, they could smell cooking in the Speaker's kitchen, and horses in one of the yards. Reid was dismissed.

Grilles in Central Lobby: The metal grilles in the ground-level windows of Central Lobby were originally in the Ladies Gallery of the Commons Chamber: before 1918, women had to watch proceedings from a separate gallery. The grilles (see left) covered the windows of the Ladies Gallery to hide women from view in case the sight of them distracted MPs. The grilles were a powerful symbol of the fact that women were not allowed to take part in Parliament. As part of the campaign for votes for women in the early 20th century, a suffragette chained herself to one of the grilles in 1908, shouting "We have listened behind this insulting grille too long!" The grille had to be removed from its frame so that the suffragettes could be cut free. The grilles were finally removed from the Ladies Gallery and installed in the windows of Central Lobby in 1917.

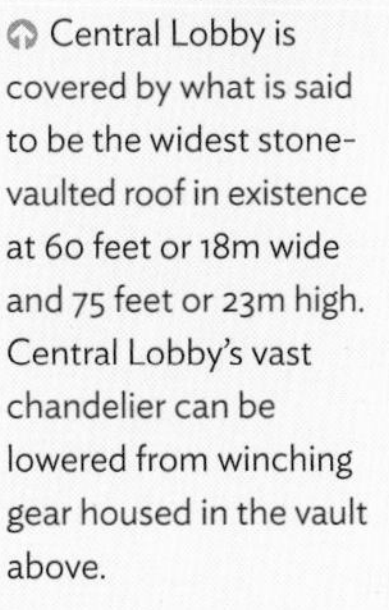

Central Lobby is covered by what is said to be the widest stone-vaulted roof in existence at 60 feet or 18m wide and 75 feet or 23m high. Central Lobby's vast chandelier can be lowered from winching gear housed in the vault above.

Lord John, 1st Earl Russell
Sir Joseph Boehm
Marble, 1880 [WOA S77]

William Ewart Gladstone
F W Pomeroy, marble, 1900 [WOAS39]

In a career lasting for more than 60 years, Gladstone (1809-98) served as Prime Minister four times and was 84 when he finally left office. The forefinger of his left hand is missing. Contrary to the rumour that he had an accident chopping wood, Gladstone injured his hand while shooting in 1842 and thereafter always wore a protective covering in place of the missing forefinger.

Commons Corridor

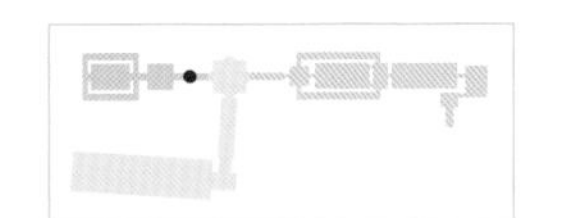

Commissioned in 1853, the murals in the Commons Corridor were painted by Edward Matthew Ward (1816-79). They depict events in the second half of the 17th century culminating in the Glorious Revolution of 1688, which established Parliament's supremacy over the monarchy. As in Peers Corridor, the Fine Arts Commission chose the subjects carefully. They focus on particular heroic acts and more intimate scenes rather than significant battles as the Commission's intention was to represent fairly both sides of the conflicts portrayed. For example, Alice Lisle is pictured concealing anti-royalist fugitives after the Battle of Sedgemoor of 1685 when the King's army defeated the rebel army led by the Duke of Monmouth, an act for which she was beheaded. The Duke of Argyll is shown sleeping the night before his execution for rebelling against the King in Scotland in 1685.

The Lords and Commons presenting the Crown to William and Mary in the Banqueting House, 1688
Edward M Ward, waterglass, 1867 [WOA 2606]

Much of the stained glass in the building was damaged or destroyed during the Second World War, including the glass in this corridor. The glass you see today was made by Hardman & Co., the same company which made the original glass. The floor tiles are replicas of the original tiles and were laid in the 1970s.

Alice Lisle Concealing the Fugitives after the Battle of Sedgemoor
Edward M Ward
Fresco, 1857
[WOA 2604]

Members Lobby

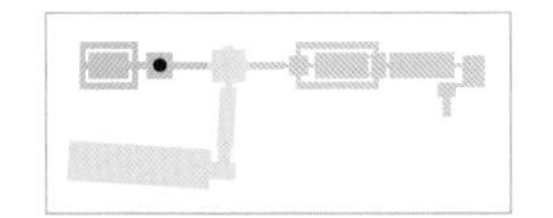

The Members Lobby is the ante-room to the House of Commons. Its roof caved in after bombing in the Second World War and the lobby was extensively damaged. The walls were rebuilt after the war but the arch leading to the Chamber is much as it was after the bombing and still shows reddish patches left by the heat of the flames. It is known as the Churchill Arch because Winston Churchill (1874-1965) suggested that it remain in its damaged state as a monument to the ordeal of the war and the fortitude of those who lived through it. The room is lit by vertical neon or fluorescent tubes in gothic-style chandeliers. Neon was a new technology at the time the lobby was rebuilt and the chandeliers exemplify how the designer, Giles Gilbert Scott (1880-1960), like Pugin before him, gave modern fittings gothic styling.

The majority of the statues in this room are of 20th century Prime Ministers and reflect a variety of sculptural styles. The specially commissioned bronze statue of Churchill by Oscar Nemon (1906-85) dominates the space. It is matched by a bronze statue of Margaret Thatcher, standing as if at the Despatch Box in the House of Commons. Also of note is Jacob Epstein's (1880-1959) bust of the first Labour Prime Minister, James Ramsay MacDonald (1866-1937).

Doorkeepers guard the entrance to the Chamber when the House is sitting. Two doorkeepers' chairs, one on either side of the Churchill Arch, contain a lever for ringing the division bells to signal a vote. The Principal Doorkeeper, who sits in the chair on the right, also traditionally keeps a box of snuff for the use of any MP, which is still requested occasionally. The box is made of oak saved from the Chamber after the Second World War. There are boards with pigeonholes for notes to be left for MPs: if a message is left, the MP's name is illuminated. The nearby Vote Office supplies MPs with parliamentary business papers.

James Ramsay MacDonald
Jacob Epstein
Bronze, 1926 [WOA S222]

The door to the Commons Chamber is worn in the place where Black Rod knocks at the State Opening of Parliament (see pages 34-5)

There is a worn area on one of the doors to the Commons Chamber. In a historic ritual associated with the State Opening of Parliament, the doors are slammed in the face of Black Rod, who comes from the House of Lords, on the monarch's behalf, to invite the MPs to listen to the monarch's speech. This is done to symbolise the Commons' independence from the monarchy. Black Rod must knock on the door three times with his staff before he is admitted. He always strikes the same part of the door.

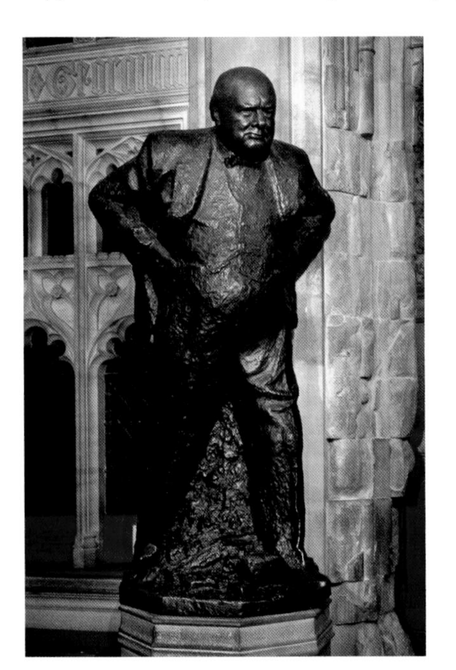

Sir Winston Churchill
Oscar Nemon
Bronze, 1969 [WOA S23]

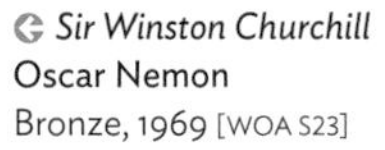

Baroness Margaret Thatcher
Antony Dufort
Bronze, 2007 [WOA S531]

“We shape our buildings, and afterwards our buildings shape us”

WINSTON CHURCHILL, on the rebuilding of the House of Commons, 1943.

Commons Chamber

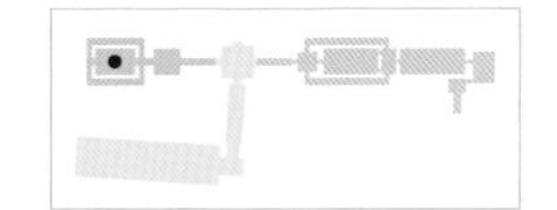

Bomb damage to the entrance to the Commons Chamber, 1941.
Parliamentary Archives, ARC/VAR/12

On 10 May 1941, at the height of the Second World War, the Commons Chamber was completely destroyed by fire after being hit by bombs (see right). The new Chamber was designed by Giles Gilbert Scott. It is smaller than many people expect, with fewer seats than there are MPs, as Winston Churchill wanted everyone present to be able to see and hear what was going on. The number of MPs has varied over time because of changes to constituency sizes and other factors, but has been over 600 since 1801. Not all MPs attend all debates, so space is not usually a problem, although it can become crowded on significant occasions such as Budget day and Prime Minister's Questions.

The Speaker chairs House of Commons debates, decides which MPs speak, and is responsible for making sure the House's rules are observed. The Speaker's original role was to act as spokesperson for the House of Commons to the monarch and the House of Lords. The Speaker still acts as the House's representative on important occasions.

The Speaker is politically impartial, so an MP elected to the post will resign from his or her political party. Although the Speaker still stands in general elections, the convention is that they are not opposed in their constituency by candidates from other parties.

The Speaker has an official residence in the Palace of Westminster called Speaker's House. Every time the House sits, the Speaker walks in a formal procession from the residence to the Commons Chamber, passing through Central Lobby. The Serjeant at Arms, who is responsible for security in the House of Commons, walks in front, carrying the Mace, and the trainbearer, chaplain and Speaker's secretary walk behind.

The first person to be called Speaker of the House of Commons in the official record of its proceedings was Thomas Hungerford (d. 1397), elected in 1377.

Speakers often had to carry unwelcome news to the monarch, which made the job rather dangerous. Nine of Sir Thomas Hungerford's successors were violently killed, seven of them by beheading.

Rt Hon. John Bercow MP
Brendan Kelly
Oil on canvas, 2011
[WOA 7212]

The Commons Chamber facing north towards the press gallery above the Speaker's Chair. The white line in the foreground denotes the Bar of the House.

Giles Gilbert Scott (1880 – 1960) was a British architect who embraced 20th century technology as well as traditional styles, such as gothic and Georgian, in his work. He is best known for Liverpool's Anglican Cathedral, which he designed at the age of 22, Battersea Power Station and Bankside Power Station, now the Tate Modern art gallery. He is also responsible for designing the UK's iconic red telephone box. Scott came from a family of architects. His grandfather, George Gilbert Scott, designed the Foreign and Commonwealth Office in Whitehall and the gothic-inspired hotel that fronts St Pancras station in London.

Sir Giles Gilbert Scott
Reginald Grenville Eves
Oil on canvas, 1935
National Portrait Gallery

Commonwealth countries contributed to the Commons when its Chamber was rebuilt after the Second World War. Most of the furniture and fittings used in the refurbishment were made in Britain, often with native woods from donor countries.

- In the Commons Chamber, Canada gave the Table of the House and South Africa gave the three chairs for the Table. Native woods were given by Australia for the Speaker's Chair and New Zealand for the two Despatch Boxes.
- Nigeria gave woods for furniture for the 'Aye' Division Lobby and Uganda for furniture for the 'No' Division Lobby. Belize, Ghana, Kenya, Newfoundland, St Helena, Sierra Leone and Tanzania also gave woods.
- Gifts also came from Zambia (bronze brackets to hold the Mace at the Table), Zimbabwe (inkstands with stationery racks on the Table), India (north entrance doors), Pakistan (south entrance doors), Jamaica (Bar of the House), Northern Ireland (the Chamber's three clocks), Sri Lanka (Serjeant at Arms' chair), Bahamas, Barbados, Bermuda, Botswana, Cyprus, Dominica, Falkland Islands, Fiji, The Gambia, Gibraltar, Grenada, Guernsey, Guyana, Hong Kong, the Isle of Man, Jersey, Leeward Islands, Lesotho, Malawi, Malaysia, Malta, Mauritius, Sabah, St Lucia, St Vincent, Seychelles, Singapore, Swaziland, Trinidad and Tobago, Yemen, and Zanzibar.

Despatch Boxes: When Ministers or shadow Ministers stand to speak in either House, they do so at the Despatch Box on their side of the table and may rest their papers on the box. No despatches are actually stored in the boxes. Instead, they contain a range of religious texts for taking the oath – the ceremony in which Members swear or affirm allegiance to the crown when they are introduced as a Member for the first time or at the start of a Parliament.

The Mace is placed beneath the Table, signalling that the Commons is in committee.

Only MPs and some parliamentary officials are allowed past the Bar of the House when the House is sitting.

The Speaker's Chair was made in Britain by H H Martyn & Co. using native black bean wood given by Australia.

Native Puriri wood from New Zealand was used to make the Despatch Boxes.

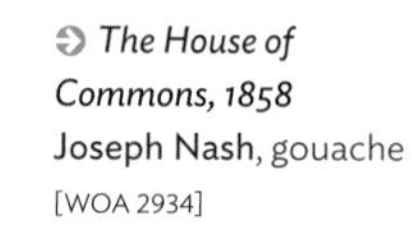

The House of Commons, 1858
Joseph Nash, gouache
[WOA 2934]

After the new Commons Chamber was first opened in 1850, Members pressed for the ceiling design to be altered to improve acoustics. This evening sitting, with Speaker Denison in the chair and Lord Palmerston addressing the House, shows the revised arrangement, and how effectively the central glazed ceiling panels, lit from behind by gas light, illuminated the Chamber.

Though gothic in design, the Chamber contrasts with the rest of the Palace as the decoration is more restrained. The wooden panelling above the gallery seating and brackets supporting the roof structure are plain, for example. Designed in the immediate postwar period at a time of rationing and austerity, the Chamber has been criticised for lacking the style of its 19th century counterpart but its predecessor was also far less ornate than the Lords Chamber.

Seating space for MPs has always been limited. Before it was destroyed in the fire of 1834, the Chamber was just under 50 ft (15m) long by 33 ft (10m) wide. It has been calculated that 342 Members could be fitted into the four rows of benches on each side and that another 150 might sit in the galleries, but before 1800 there was not even standing room for a full House of 558 MPs. Today, the Chamber is just under 70 ft (21m) long by 46 ft (14m) wide and provides seating for an estimated 437 MPs (including seating in the galleries).

Division Lobbies: Votes in the Commons and the Lords are known as divisions. At the end of a debate in the Chamber, the Speaker in the Commons and the Lord Speaker in the Lords usually asks the opinion of Members on the question, called a motion, under debate. If there is disagreement, bells sound throughout parliamentary buildings to summon Members. The House 'divides' and everyone wishing to vote leaves the Chamber and goes into the Division Lobbies. MPs who support the motion go into the Aye Lobby; those who oppose it go into the No Lobby. Members vote by giving their name to clerks. They then leave the lobbies past two Members who act as tellers, counting the votes. The tellers announce the result to the Chamber. In the House of Lords, votes cast in agreement with the motion are known as Contents, and those against as Not Contents.

The House of Commons in Session, 1986
June Mendoza, oil on canvas, 1987 [WOA 3232]

Margaret Thatcher addresses a packed House of Commons Chamber in July 1986 at Prime Minister's Question Time. Neil Kinnock, Leader of the Opposition leans forward prominently on the Opposition front bench. With so many portraits to paint, it took the artist over fifteen months to complete this commission.

The 19 coats of arms along the south gallery commemorate MPs who died in the First World War, and the 23 opposite along the northern gallery those who died in the Second World War. Shields above the north and south entrances bear the arms of four MPs who were killed by the Irish National Liberation Army (INLA) and the Irish Republican Army (IRA).

Airey Neave was a victim of the Northern Ireland conflict, assassinated in 1979 by an INLA car bomb at the House of Commons.

This English oak crown is one of few decorative elements as the Chamber was designed in keeping with austere conditions after the Second World War.

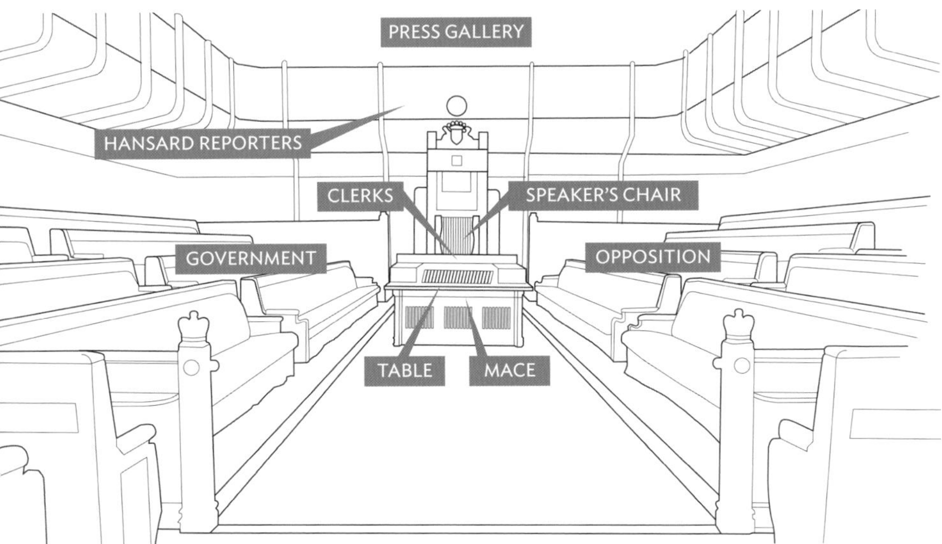

The Commons Chamber seen from the Bar of the House, directly below the public gallery from which members of the public can watch proceedings.

Parliament and the press

More than 300 journalists are accredited to the two Houses of Parliament, and about 170 have offices in the Palace. Speaker Abbot gave the press reserved seats in the Commons in 1803, and purpose-built galleries containing allocated seating were placed above both Chambers when they were rebuilt in the mid-19th century. Apart from the weekly Prime Minister's Questions, the galleries are these days rarely full as newspapers no longer provide full reports of what is said in the Chambers. Instead, proceedings can be read online. They are all webcast, and many are also televised. Users of social media increasingly report on what happens in and around Parliament as well as the print and broadcast media. Most work is done behind the scenes, including daily 'lobby' briefings by government media officers in rooms behind the Chamber.

Sword lines and the Bar of the House

The green carpet on the floor of the Chamber of the House of Commons is marked by a red line in front of each of the two banks of benches, and there is a white line across the width of the House at its entrance. The red lines are known as sword lines, supposedly because they are designed to keep MPs on opposing sides two sword lengths apart. This is only a myth, however: swords have never been allowed in the Chamber. Those speaking from the front benches may not step beyond their sword line. The white line marks the position of the Bar of the House, which only MPs or some parliamentary officials may pass when the House is sitting. The Bar of the House in the Lords is a rail, at which the Members of the House of Commons gather to hear the Queen's Speech.

St Stephen's Hall

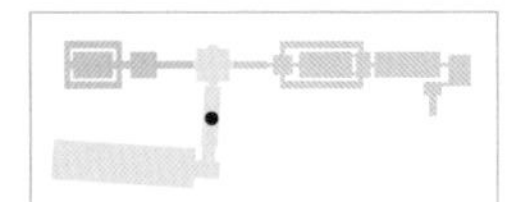

St Stephen's Hall is on the site where the House of Commons sat from the mid-16th century until the fire of 1834. It stands on the site of the royal chapel of St Stephen which was destroyed in the fire, but retains the shape and dimensions of the original chapel. Its stained glass windows and murals seek to restore some of the colour for which it was once famous.

St Stephen's was the site of great parliamentary events for nearly 300 years. Famous orators such as Walpole, Pitt and Fox, debated here; William Wilberforce (1759–1833) argued against the slave trade; and it was here that Charles I tried to arrest five Members of the House of Commons only to be confronted by the Speaker, William Lenthall. The statues commissioned for the hall reflect its earlier role and depict in marble the great parliamentary orators. The statue of Lord Falkland (d. 1643) has a spur from one boot

St Stephen's Hall facing east towards Central Lobby. The Hall retains the layout and many of the qualities of the chapel which used to occupy this site. The mosaic above the door shows St Stephen.

Richard I leaving England for the Crusades
Glyn Warren Philpot, oil on canvas, 1925–27 [WOA 2601]

British history is the common theme for the murals in St Stephen's Hall. In this painting, Richard I represents those who have fought valiantly for the country and helped to shape the nation over the centuries.

missing: the damage was caused in 1909 when a suffragette chained herself to the statue in protest against the refusal to grant women the right to vote.

Members used the original chapel choir stalls, which meant that politicians on either side were facing each other. The debating rooms in the Palace today, including Commons and Lords Chambers, are still laid out like this. Some Committee Rooms are arranged in a 'horseshoe' pattern instead so that the whole Committee can see and be seen by the people from whom they are taking evidence. A similar horseshoe layout was introduced in the Westminster Hall debating chamber in 1999, but MPs from different political parties still tend to sit facing each other across the room. Today, the only seats which remain in St Stephen's Hall are stone benches integrated into the walls which visitors may use when waiting to enter the public gallery to listen to debates.

Four brass studs in the floor mark where the Speaker's Chair stood and, before that, the chapel's altar. Nearby, four studs in a square mark the position of the original Table which held the Mace. Two brass tablets in the side walls, about 30ft (9m) from the west end, mark the position of a wall which separated the Lobby from the Chamber: this Chamber was much smaller than the current one.

The Hall's 10 stained glass windows show the coats of arms of cities and boroughs. The statues were installed in the 19th century but the decorations were completed only in the 1920s when the murals were painted and the mosaics installed.

The murals illustrate *The Building of Britain* and were privately funded by members of the House of Lords. JH Whitley, Speaker of the Commons 1921-28, who oversaw the work, wanted the murals to appeal to *"the ordinary citizen and to the schoolchildren who visit the home of their Parliament"*. Their subjects chart over 800 years of British history, from when King Alfred's longships defended the realm in the late 9th century to the Union of England and Scotland in 1707.

The mosaics above the two entrance arches relate to St Stephen. Over the entrance to Central Lobby, St Stephen is depicted standing between a crowned soldier, King Stephen, and a crowned saint, Edward the Confessor, symbolising the strength and aspiration of good government. Opposite, Edward III is shown commanding the construction of St Stephen's chapel. Kneeling before him is his Master Mason, Thomas of Canterbury. The model for the mason was a member of staff in Parliament, Thomas Wilson, the Clerk of Works who oversaw the installation of the mosaics.

The Dearsley Bequest stained glass windows designed by Shona McInnes.

Mrs Dearsley, a great admirer of the Palace of Westminster, left a bequest in 1995 to be spent on the building. Eight modern stained glass windows were commissioned to illustrate the development of the democratic franchise from the 'Model Parliament' called by Edward I in 1295 to the lowering of the voting age to 18 in 1969 and devolution in 1998.

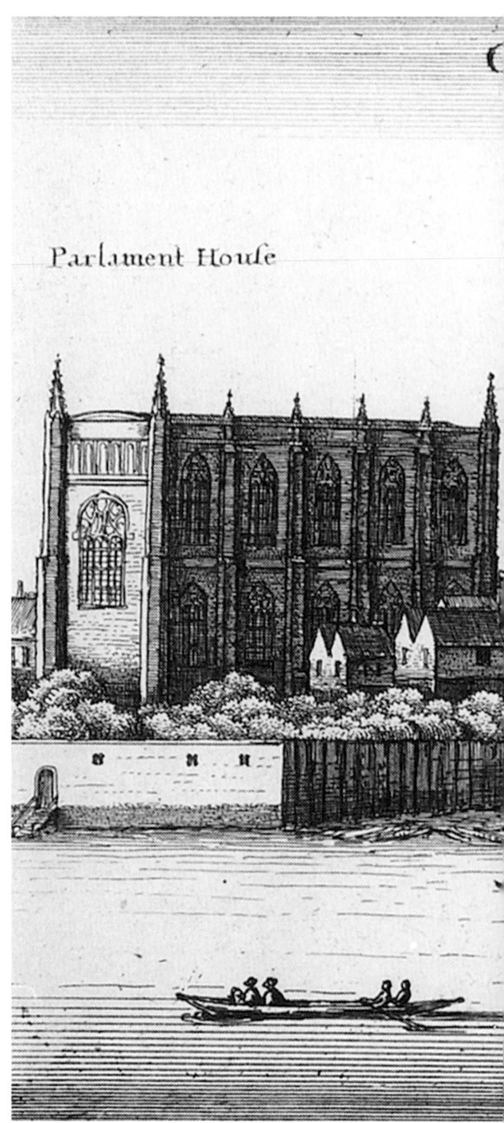

Westminster, 1647
Wenceslaus Hollar
Etching, 1647 [WOA 845]

A view of the north bank of the Thames, showing the 'Parlament House' (St Stephen's Chapel), 'the Hall' (Westminster Hall) and 'the Abby' (Westminster Abbey).

Speaker John Henry Whitley
Glyn Philpot
Oil on canvas, 1929
[WOA 3226]

Speaker Whitley stands at the doorway to St Stephen's Hall, the newly completed *Building of Britain* series visible behind him, including Philpot's mural of Richard I.

The vault of St Stephen's Hall was constructed to simulate the 14th century wooden vault of St Stephen's Chapel which stood on this site. Carved bosses show subjects taken from the life of St Stephen. The brass chandeliers were made after the fire in 1834 for the temporary Commons Chamber while the new Palace was being constructed.

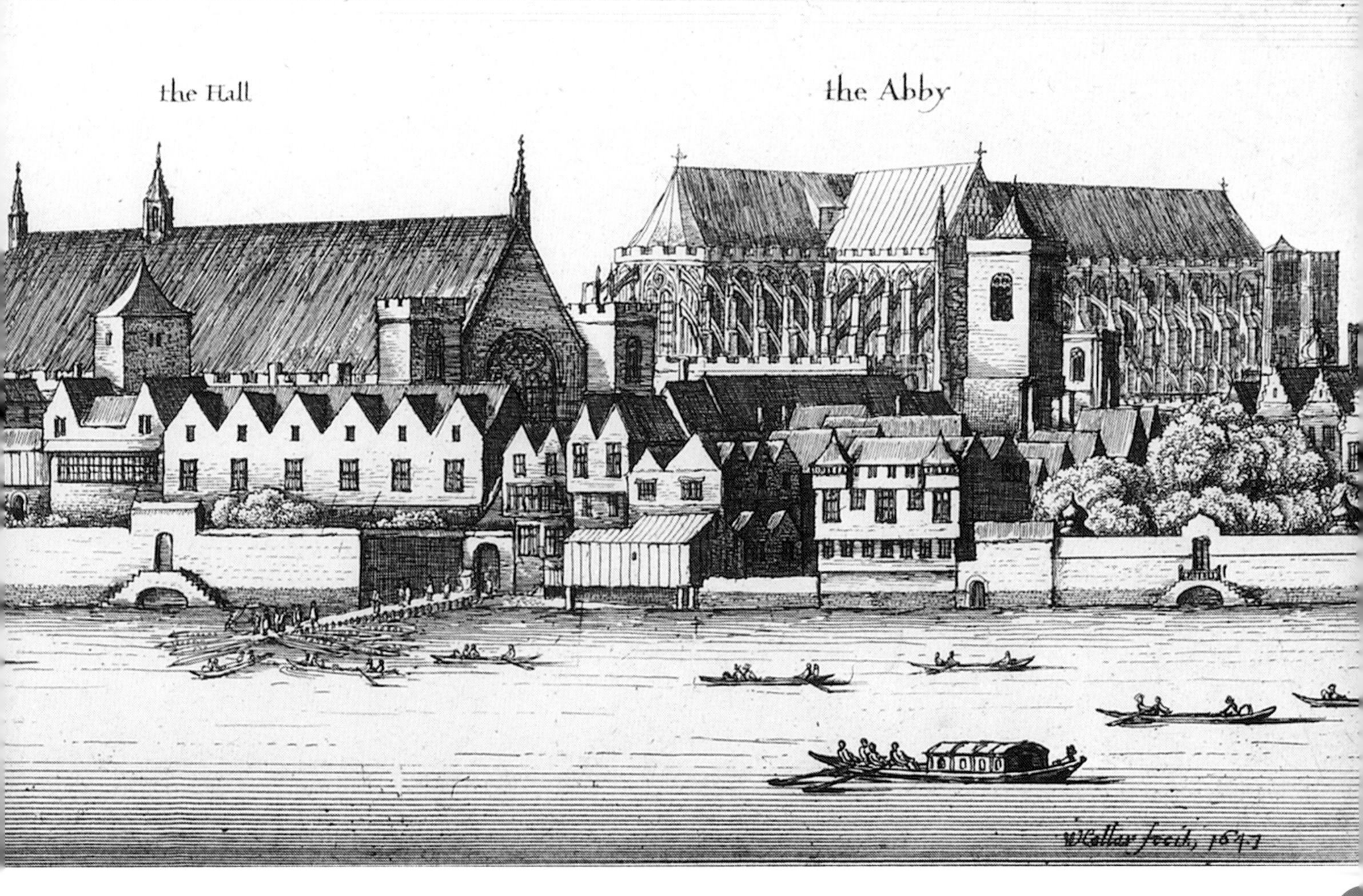

Westminster Hall

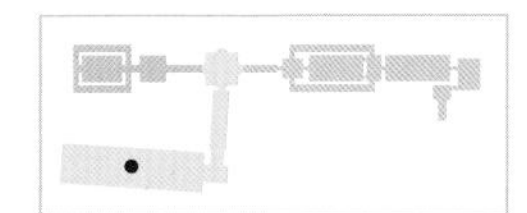

In October 1834, when a devastating fire spread through the Palace, Westminster Hall, which had played a central part in the nation's history, was saved at the expense of most of the rest of the medieval palace. Again in 1941, when fire from wartime bombs threatened both the Commons Chamber and the Hall, the Hall was saved.

Westminster Hall is the oldest part of the Palace of Westminster. Standing in the Hall today, you mainly see elements that were added in the centuries after it was first built in the reign of William II (d. 1100). The lower walls, over 6ft (1.8m) thick, for the most part date from then, but Richard II remodelled the Hall in the 14th century into its present form, and nearly all the visible stonework dates from the 19th century.

THE HAMMER-BEAM ROOF

Work on the most striking element, the timber roof, started in 1393. The roof is the largest hammer-beam roof in the world and the largest medieval unsupported roof in northern Europe. Thanks to its design, no pillars were needed in the Hall itself, creating the huge, uninterrupted space that is still used for state occasions, and which would have astounded early visitors. A new steel structure was inserted in the early 20th century to provide support, and a little under 10% of the timber was replaced, using oak from Wadhurst in Kent, some of it from trees that were already fully-grown when the original roof was built.

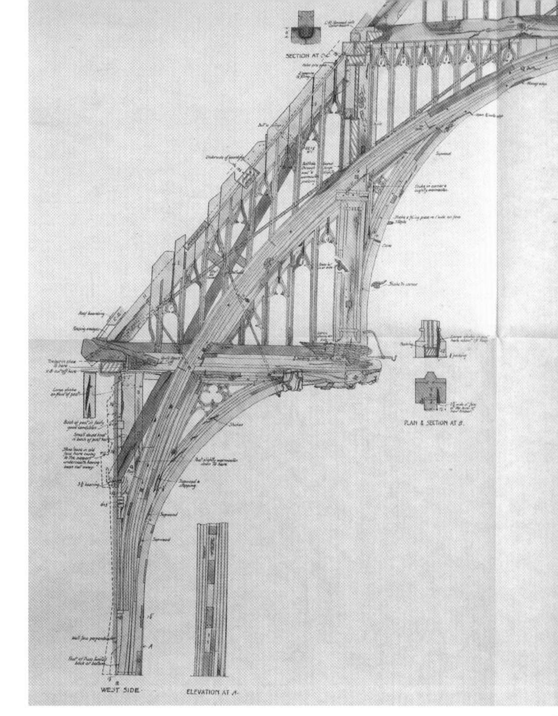

Detail of Westminster Hall roof truss
Sir Frank Baines, 1914.
Parliamentary Archives, HC/LB/1/114/42

The North Façade of Westminster Hall
attributed to Thomas Sandby
Oil on canvas, *c.* 1795 [WOA 2271]

Two imposing stone towers flank the arched entrance to Westminster Hall. They were part of the 14th century remodelling of the Hall. By the late 18th century a collection of pubs and coffee houses were to be found at the base of the towers.

Firefighting in Westminster Hall on the Night of the Fire in 1834
G B Campion, watercolour, 1834 [WOA 1669]

Firefighters managed to save the medieval roof timbers of Westminster Hall by dousing them with water. It was a scene of high drama and frenetic activity as teams of men worked the water pumps.

Westminster Hall is the oldest and, at 239ft by 68ft (73m by 21m), largest room in the Palace. Over 600 tonnes of oak were used to make its 14th century roof. Visitors at the time would never have seen a ceiling this big without pillars holding it up.

Interior of Westminster Hall
J Bluck after A C Pugin , etching, 1809 [WOA 3835]

William Kent's gothic screen, installed in the mid 18th century, was a significant structure inside Westminster Hall. It separated two of the Law Courts from the rest of the Hall.

The chained hart or stag was the motif of Richard II.

ROYAL EMBLEMS

The architecture incorporates further decorative reminders of the Hall's royal history: 26 carved angels form the lower part of the roof's timber frame and bear the royal arms of the time: the fleur de lys of France and the three lions of England. A frieze of Richard II's badge of chained harts (stags) runs below the windows. The statues of kings on the south wall were carved in 1385 and would originally have been brightly painted and gilded. They are not likenesses of individual monarchs, but rather images of medieval kingship dressed in robes of the late 14th century court.

The stained glass window in the south wall was designed by the architect, Ninian Comper (1864-1960), and contains the arms and monograms of MPs, peers and staff of the Commons and the Lords who died in the Second World War, along with the badges of their regiment, squadron or ship.

USAGE OF WESTMINSTER HALL

Westminster Hall was, and still is, the scene of great state ceremonies, including the lying in state of monarchs. In the past, many famous state trials, royal councils and coronation feasts also took place here. Plaques in the floor of the Hall and steps leading up to St Stephen's Porch commemorate many of these significant events. Today, the Hall continues to be used for state ceremonies and parliamentary exhibitions.

Coronation banquet of George IV in Westminster Hall
by an unknown artist
Oil on paper, c. 1821 [WOA 5870]

The pomp and ceremony of George IV's coronation banquet transformed Westminster Hall. Guests lined the walls in specially erected side galleries. Tables of diners extended the full length of the Hall, with the King and his entourage seated on an elevated platform at the south end.

The Lying in State – Close View – The Life Guards
Hugh Buchanan
Watercolour, 2002 [WOA 5959]

On her death, Queen Elizabeth, the Queen Mother and George VI's widow was honoured with a lying in state. Over three days in 2002, some 200,000 people came to pay their respects. Other monarchs and their consorts who have had a lying in state in Westminster Hall are: Edward VII (1910), George V (1936), George VI (1952), and Queen Mary, the widow of George V (1953). Winston Churchill was also given the honour in 1965.

Cast brass figures of a lion representing England and a dragon representing Wales appear on candelabra reproduced in the 1970s from drawings of the lost originals.

ROYAL AND STATE CEREMONIES

The earliest recorded coronation feasts to take place in Westminster Hall were those of Prince Henry (1155-83) in 1170 and of Richard I in 1189. The festivities after the coronation of George IV (1762-1830) in 1821 were extraordinarily lavish and the practice was discontinued in 1830 by William IV (1765-1837) as an unwarranted expense.

Several monarchs and their consorts and great parliamentarians have been given a lying in state in Westminster Hall. The lying in state is a formal occasion in which the public can come and pay their respects to the deceased before a funeral ceremony. The coffin is placed on a raised platform in the middle of the Hall and a guard of honour is in attendance 24 hours a day.

Former Prime Minister, William Ewart Gladstone, was the first to be given the honour in 1898. An unusual lying in state took place for a single day in 1930 when some 90,000 people came to pay their respects to the 48 victims of the R101 airship crash.

Westminster Hall is still used on ceremonial occasions. The House of Commons and House of Lords presented ceremonial addresses to Queen Elizabeth II here to congratulate her on her Silver Jubilee in 1977, her Golden Jubilee in 2002 and her Diamond Jubilee in 2012 when Members of both Houses presented her with a stained glass window to be mounted in the north window. Visiting Heads of State, including President Nelson Mandela, Pope Benedict XVI and U.S. President Barack Obama, have addressed Members of both Houses of Parliament here.

The Trial of Charles I in Westminster Hall
John Nalson, *engraving, 1688* [WOA 7166]
The trial of Charles I on 4 January 1649.

LAW COURTS

Monarchs used Westminster Hall as a law court, often sitting in judgment themselves. Law courts were based in and around the Hall from the end of the 13th century until 1882. The court of the King's Bench, one of the highest law courts, which occupied a corner at the south end of Westminster Hall, was so named because the king originally presided there. Even when monarchs were not present, a throne and high table symbolised their authority. It occupied a central position at the south end of Westminster Hall.

These courts were semi-permanent structures. A large gothic screen was constructed in 1740 by the architect, William Kent (1685-1748), to separate two of the courts from the open public area of the Hall, which included booksellers' shops and refreshment stalls. These structures often had to be taken down to allow the Hall to be used for other events. For major state trials, a temporary court was constructed, usually with large viewing stands for the public. Permanent courts were built to the west of the Hall in the 1820s. These were dismantled in 1882, when the Royal Courts of Justice opened in the Strand.

FAMOUS TRIALS

One famous early trial was that of William Wallace (d. 1305) who led Scottish resistance to the English King Edward I in the 1290s. As an outlaw, Wallace was not allowed to defend himself, and he was sentenced to be hung, drawn and quartered. He has long been celebrated as a hero of Scottish independence.

No. 84
Joseph Gurney
For the Trial of Warren Hastings Esq.
Permit the Bearer to Pafs and Repafs.
(NOT TRANSFERABLE)

Pass for Joseph Gurney, shorthand reporter, to attend the trial of Warren Hastings, 1789.
Parliamentary Archives, HL/PO/LB/1/55

The Trial of Warren Hastings 1788-1795 by an unknown artist, engraving [WOA 2818]

The former Speaker and Lord Chancellor Sir Thomas More (1478-1535) was tried for treason in Westminster Hall. When Henry VIII decided to divorce his first wife, Catherine of Aragon, he triggered a constitutional and religious crisis that culminated in the creation of the Church of England. More refused to recognise Henry VIII as the Supreme Head of the Church. He was executed at the Tower of London. More was canonised by the Roman Catholic Church in 1935.

The trial of Guy Fawkes and seven other men involved in the Gunpowder Plot took place in Westminster Hall on 27 January 1606. All eight were found guilty of treason for attempting to kill King James I and sentenced to death. Guy Fawkes and three others were executed in Old Palace Yard on 31 January 1606.

Charles I was tried in the Hall at the end of the Civil War, in 1649. He was found guilty of waging war against Parliament and people. For three days, he refused to recognise the court, claiming that it had no authority over him. However, the judges overruled him, and he was sentenced to death. The original death warrant is in the Parliamentary Archives, and a copy is on display in the Royal Gallery. Charles I was beheaded in Whitehall on 30 January 1649.

Westminster Hall was sometimes used to hold impeachments and trials of Ministers or other major public officials. The most notorious was the impeachment of Warren Hastings (1732-1818) for corruption during his time as Governor-General of Bengal. The trial lasted, on and off, from 1788 to 1795, and ended with his acquittal.

The First Day of Term
Charles Mosley *after* Hubert Gravelot
Engraving, 1738 [WOA 673]

A view of Westminster Hall on the first day of the legal term in 1738, with lawyers talking to their clients. The Courts of King's Bench and Chancery are visible at the south wall, either side of the steps; the Court of Common Pleas is at the west wall, with bookstalls nearby.

Westminster Hall debating chamber
The Grand Committee Room off the north-west corner of Westminster Hall has been used since 1999 by the House of Commons to debate select committee reports and general subjects of interest nominated by MPs. This helps relieve the pressure on debating time in the main Commons Chamber.

During the Second World War, the Palace of Westminster was damaged 14 times by air raids, most severely on 10 May 1941, when bombs fell on the Commons Chamber, and the roof of Westminster Hall caught fire. It was impossible to save both, so Westminster Hall was preserved because of its historical importance. The Commons met in the Lords Chamber and the Lords met in the Robing Room until the Chamber was rebuilt in 1950. Arrangements were made for Parliament to sit outside London if necessary, although it never actually did so.

The King's High Table was a symbol of royal might, used for more than 400 years by kings and queens including Henry V (1386-1422) and Elizabeth I (1533-1603). At the table, the kings and queens were acclaimed by the Lords before being crowned in Westminster Abbey and afterwards it was used for the coronation feast. The table was broken up in the 17th century but fragments of it were discovered in 2005. Made of Purbeck marble from Dorset, the table was built as a series of uprights delicately carved with a gothic arch and round column. The excavation of one of its legs is pictured below.

The Chapel of St Mary Undercroft is under St Stephen's Hall. It was built between 1292 and 1297, and the Court and royal household worshipped there. Over the years, it stopped being used for worship, and was pressed into service at different times as a wine cellar, a dining room for the Speaker (holes were bored into the wall to accommodate the kitchen chimneys) and a stable for Oliver Cromwell's horses (although no formal record survives confirming this). The chapel was one of the few parts of the Palace of Westminster to survive the fire of 1834 more or less intact, although a lot of the stonework was damaged.

The chapel was decorated in the 1860s by Edward Barry. Gilded, painted and stencilled designs in rich colours cover the walls, floor and vaulting. The backdrop to the altar depicts royal British saints. Religious services are held in the chapel.

The organ was made by William Drake of Buckfastleigh in Devon, and installed in 1999. Its case is based on a previously unexecuted design by Pugin. The stencil patterns were devised by John Bucknall, and the painted doors were by Fleur Kelly.

The Chapel of St Mary Undercroft
Edward Middleton Barry
Watercolour, circa 1863 [WOA 1601]

E M Barry's Victorian designs for sumptuous gilded and painted decoration for the interior of the chapel are clearly illustrated in this watercolour. Work on the chapel was finished in 1865.

Decorative details include carved medieval ceiling bosses (above) and the cast brass relief of an angel on the pulpit (right) which was made by Hardman & Co., and represents St Matthew.

The chapel's elaborate decorations shine to jewel-like effect. The vault painting and gold leaf was done by F D Crace and Clayton and Bell.

Edward Barry designed the baptistery and the font, the basin of which is a single block of alabaster.

Heritage

Few buildings in the world generate as much interest and admiration as the Palace of Westminster. This is a testament to the work of Charles Barry (1795–1860) who designed it, and to its role in the nation's history.

The Palace is part of the Westminster UNESCO World Heritage Site which also incorporates Westminster Abbey, the Jewel Tower and St Margaret's Church, yet it is also home to a working Parliament. A large team of people is dedicated to the challenges not only of conserving its many treasures but of ensuring that it is fit for purpose as a 21st century workplace.

Victoria Tower
Frank O Salisbury, oil on canvas [WOA 6588]

A view of Victoria Tower during the 1930s taken from a scaffold around the Central Tower.

ARCHITECTURE AND DESIGN
Following the fire in 1834, a national competition was held to design the new Palace of Westminster. The designs were to be in the gothic or Elizabethan style, and located on the original site. There were 97 entries and the winner of the competition, Charles Barry, was announced in 1836.

Barry's design combines classical planning and picturesque outline. The building's regular bays, with identical towered pavilions projecting at north and south ends, are broken up by three asymmetrically placed towers: the Clock Tower, Central Tower and Victoria Tower.

THE BUILDING
Inspiration for the design of the Palace's façades came from the ornate 16th century Henry VII chapel in Westminster Abbey. The silhouette of the building against the skyline is a mixture of towers, battlements, pinnacles, other detailed stonework, flags, steep roofs of Flemish inspiration, and royal symbols such as crowns.

The details of the façades vary from section to section. Rows of statues representing monarchs are inserted between the windows. Panels with royal symbols, shields or other carvings mark the position of the floors. The sculptor and architect John Thomas (1813-62) superintended all the stone carving and was responsible for producing the statues of kings and queens both on the exterior and inside the Palace.

The major feature of the layout is the Palace's north-south spine which, on the principal floor, links the main rooms. Starting from the south, these are the Queen's Robing Room, the Royal Gallery, the Prince's Chamber, the House of Lords Chamber, Central Lobby and House of Commons Chamber. A succession of courtyards helps to bring light into corridors and offices although some courtyards became smaller as new buildings were added.

View of the Palace of Westminster with the Victoria Tower under Construction
by an unknown artist, oil on board [WOA 6480]

In this painting the scaffold used to construct it is clearly visible on top of the partially built tower.

The Victoria Tower of the Houses of Parliament seen from Parliament Square, 1893
John Crowther, watercolour, 1893 [WOA 3632]

When Victoria Tower was completed, it dominated the surrounding buildings.

Charles Barry (1795–1860) spent 25 years designing and constructing the Palace of Westminster between 1835 and 1860. Barry was born across the road from where the Clock Tower now stands, on Bridge Street, and baptised in St Margaret's, Westminster. Designing and building the Palace of Westminster was an enormous undertaking by any standards and it is a tribute to Barry's powers as superintending architect that he drove the project forward so skilfully. His romantic vision of a gothic Palace to house the Parliament of the wealthiest nation in the world took over 20 years to achieve. Working very long hours to satisfy demanding committees, Barry patiently developed a plan to accommodate the many and various functions of the legislature.

His third son, Edward, also an architect, was chosen to complete his father's work in the ten years after his death.

Charles Barry's other notable works include the Reform Club on Pall Mall and the Athenaeum in Manchester which is now part of the City Art Gallery. He also remodelled Trafalgar Square and rebuilt the old Treasury (now Cabinet Office) building on Whitehall.

Charles Barry
Henry William Pickersgill
Oil on canvas, 19th century [WOA 2729]

The Palace's long terrace links the building to the river, which was still a busy transport artery linking London to the rest of the world in the mid 19th century. Building materials for the Palace were brought by river in red-sailed sloops.

The Palace's roof was a major 19th century engineering feat and the first time galvanized cast iron roof tiles were used in the UK. Barry designed iron beams to support both the visible timber ceilings as well as an upper fireproof roof. This roof has proved astonishingly durable, only requiring an overhaul after 150 years.

Libraries and Committee Rooms are arranged on separate floors along the river frontage. The impressively long Committee Corridor on the first floor is broken up by the carved oak frames of its doorways. Its wood-panelled ceiling is, unusually for the Palace, undecorated.

The first floor Committee Corridor is reached using the Committee staircase at the foot of which is a statue of Charles Barry by J H Foley which was commissioned by the Royal Institute of British Architects in 1865 and funded by public subscription. The Committee Rooms themselves contain many of the original fireplaces, fittings, furniture and wood panelling designed by Barry and Pugin alongside modern equipment such as webcams, microphones and information screens. Selected paintings from the Parliamentary Art Collection hang on the walls.

The rebuilding of the Commons Chamber after the Second World War was entrusted to the architect Giles Gilbert Scott (see page 55), who in addition to his architectural work was also the designer of the UK's distinctive red telephone box. The new buildings were faced internally and externally with Clipsham stone from Rutland.

The New Palace at Westminster, 1851
E. Walker after **Charles Barry**, lithograph [WOA 742]

Based on Barry's architectural designs, this perspective showed how the fine exteriors of the Palace would look when it was completed. Images such as this catered to the great public appetite for information about the building under construction.

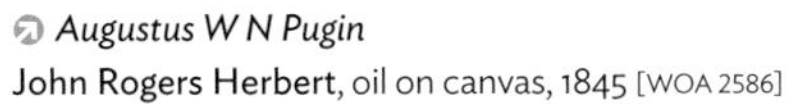

Augustus W N Pugin
John Rogers Herbert, oil on canvas, 1845 [WOA 2586]

Indian army officers, attending the coronation of King Edward VII in July 1902, on the Terrace of the House of Commons.

Parliamentary Archives, HC/LB/1/111/20/10

Augustus Welby Northmore Pugin (1812–52) was the leading exponent of the Gothic Revival style of architecture in the Victorian era. A Roman Catholic, he regarded it not only as a national style but one which had a moral dimension and which promoted a Christian way of life through the style of the Middle Ages. His writings were greatly influential.

As a young man, he travelled widely in Europe, sketching and studying gothic ornament. The understanding he developed as a result made him an obvious choice when Barry was looking for an expert to help with the multitude of detailed designs required for the Palace of Westminster's interiors. Between 1844 and his death in 1852 he worked for Barry, generating thousands of design drawings. His role also involved dealing directly with the key manufacturers, Herbert Minton, John Gregory Crace and John Hardman, to ensure that tiles, stained glass, brasswork and other decorative features of the highest standard were produced.

"I never worked so hard in my life [as] for Mr Barry for tomorrow I render all the designs for finishing his bell tower & it is beautiful".

The Clock Tower

The Clock Tower is the Palace of Westminster's most recognisable feature, rising 315 ft (96m) above the north end of the building. The chimes of four of the bells housed in its belfry ring out every quarter of an hour. The fifth, and most famous, Big Ben, strikes the hour.

Big Ben is a nickname which strictly speaking refers to the largest of the bells – the hour bell – in the Clock Tower, not to the tower itself. No one is sure where the name came from, but one suggestion is that it was named for Sir Benjamin Hall (1802-67), an MP who was First Commissioner of Works 1855-58. Another suggestion is that the workmen who made the bell named it after Benjamin Caunt, who was a famous prize fighter at that time.

When it was first designed in 1856, Big Ben was to be the largest bell ever cast in Britain. The bell that hangs in the Clock Tower is the second to have been cast after the first was broken up because it cracked during testing. It was cast in 1858 at what is now the Whitechapel Bell Foundry. It weighs 13,760 kg, which is more than 13 tons, is 7ft 6in (2.3m) high and 9ft (2.7m) in diameter and is 8¾in (22.2cm) thick at the point where it is struck. Cheering crowds lined the streets of London to watch as Big Ben was transported to the Palace of Westminster on a trolley pulled by sixteen horses. The bell had to be hauled by hand up the 200ft (60m) to the belfry in the Clock Tower, a process that took 18 hours. On 31 May 1859, Big Ben and the other bells rang out across London for the first time. The musical note Big Ben strikes is an 'E'.

Big Ben the Largest Bell Ever Cast in England
Edward Lewis & Co., lithograph, 1857 [WOA 1414]

Old penny coins are used to keep the clock accurate to within one second a day. Adding a penny will cause the clock to gain two-fifths of a second in 24 hours. Adjustment is needed from time to time because of the effects of temperature fluctuation on the metal of such a long pendulum.

The lantern at the top of the Clock Tower is known as the Ayrton Light and is lit when either House of Parliament is sitting after dark. Originally lit by gas and only visible towards west London, it is said that Queen Victoria looked at it from Buckingham Palace to check whether Members were "at work". The light was installed in 1885, and has been electric since 1903. It is named after Acton Smee Ayrton MP (1816-86), who was First Commissioner of Works at the time of its installation.

The clock face is huge: the hour hands are 9ft (2.75m) long and the minute hands are 14ft (4.27m) long . Each year, the tips of the minute hands travel 118 miles (190km). In a remarkable display of 19th century engineering, the clock is accurate to within one second, even today. The mechanism is adjusted by means of old pennies; adding one penny makes the clock gain two fifths of a second in 24 hours. One of the clock's keepers is stationed in the Clock Tower on Remembrance Sunday in November and on New Year's Eve, when it is especially important that the clock chimes on time.

Each clock face is set with 312 panes of opalescent glass.

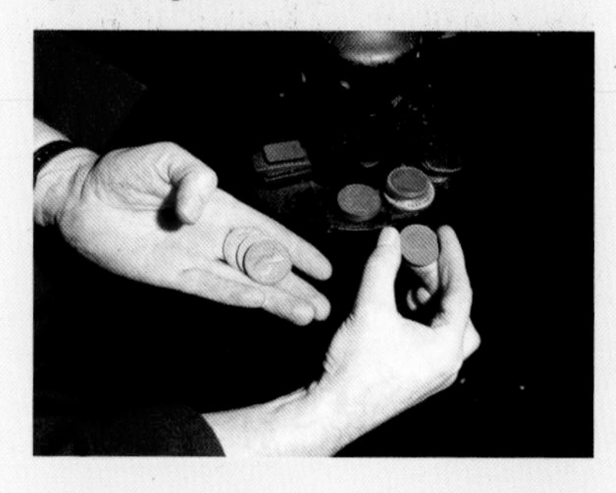

The Clock Tower has a small but noticeable tilt of 0.26 degrees. A spiral staircase of 334 steps rises inside the tower to the belfry and several small rooms are built into the lower part.

The Westminster Chimes are broadcast on BBC radio. They are a familiar sound whether they are heard at the beginning of a news bulletin or while counting in the New Year. The tune is said to be based on the aria *'I Know That My Redeemer Liveth'* in Handel's *'Messiah'*. They are also known as the Cambridge Chimes because the church of Great St Mary's in Cambridge first used the tune for its bells.

The five-tonne clock mechanism must be wound three times a week, always by hand, and this takes 20 minutes.

Victoria Tower

Victoria Tower at 323ft (98.5m) was once the tallest square tower and the tallest secular building in the world. It was named the King's Tower in the original plans after William IV, who was the reigning monarch at the time the Palace burned down in 1834.

The Victoria Tower was principally designed to house the records of Parliament. Between 1948 and 1963, the interior was redesigned to provide 12 floors of air-conditioned storage and it was further brought up to professional standards for the storage of records between 2000 and 2004.

The tower's brick core and stone exterior were built without any external scaffolding. The material was instead hoisted up through the middle of the tower by steam winch.

The central well in the vault above the Sovereign's Entrance is still used during the State Opening of Parliament. The monarch's coach stops immediately beneath it and a signal is relayed to the top of the tower to lower the Union flag and raise the Royal Standard, which signals the monarch's presence. A Union flag has flown from Victoria Tower every day since January 2010. Before then, it only flew on days when either House was sitting.

Victoria Tower flagmen, 1905.

Parliamentary Archives, FAR/1

The Act Room, Victoria Tower.
The Parliamentary Archives has responsibility for the archives of both Houses of Parliament which are stored within the Victoria Tower.

Portcullis House

Portcullis House was the first major purpose-built addition to the parliamentary estate since Giles Gilbert Scott rebuilt the Commons Chamber after the Second World War, and was designed to provide much-needed office accommodation. Opened in 2001, it incorporates Westminster Underground station beneath it and a direct route through to the Palace. It is accessible to the public on guided tours and for attending select committee proceedings.

Portcullis House echoes its more famous neighbour in various ways. For example, its façade, like that of the Palace, is divided into regular bays. The arched glass and timber roof of its atrium is inspired by that of Westminster Hall. Many of the same materials are used in its construction, both inside and out, including bronze, oak and stone. In other ways Portcullis House is unmistakably modern. Besides its more contemporary appearance, the building is mainly naturally heated and cooled. Committee rooms on the first floor feature wave-shaped ceilings that increase the building's thermal mass to help keep temperatures down in the summer, and light shelves over the bay windows reduce glare. Fountains and plants reduce noise in the main atrium and triple-glazed windows ensure the noise of traffic does not disturb users.

Portcullis House is built using Cornish granite and Derbyshire sandstone columns on a concrete frame. The design incorporates an unpowered air conditioning system which uses the 14 bronze chimneys to draw air through the building.

The New Parliamentary Building under Construction – Construction of the Glazed Roof
Gus Cummins, watercolour, 1999 [WOA 5465]

A scene of intense activity, this shows the latter stages of construction, with large prefabricated sections of roof being hoisted into position around the central glazed atrium.

Building conservation and maintenance

The Palace of Westminster requires careful conservation and maintenance and a team of experts is on hand to do the necessary work. Conservation architects, interior design and furnishings experts, project managers, engineers, fire safety and environment officers carry out special repairs and maintain the fabric of the building. The Palace's specialist crafts team includes carpenters, electricians, plumbers, carpet fitters, painters, porters, locksmiths and clock mechanics. Alterations and repairs to the building's architecture and historic interiors are carefully monitored, and as the Palace and its fittings are listed Grade I, they are also protected by law.

Conserving the stone of the Palace's exterior is a continuing challenge. The exterior suffered badly from London's pollution in the 19th and early 20th centuries which eroded the Anston stone used for most of the building. Between 1928 and 1960, some of the exterior masonry and statues were replaced. A second programme of stone cleaning and repair started in 1981. The exterior was tackled first and work continues on the inner courtyards.

Putting up the Painted Panels
Susan Henderson, oil on paper, 1984 [WOA 2854]

In July 1980 one of the carved ceiling bosses in the Chamber fell down whilst the House of Lords was meeting. Luckily no one was injured. An inspection found the ceiling to be in need of extensive restoration as it was found to have been weakened by heat from the old gas lighting. Here the work is nearing completion, with the painted panels being fixed back into position.

Installing decorations in the Royal Gallery.

Craftspeople put the finishing touches to the Throne in the Lords Chamber in preparation for the State Opening of Parliament.

An inspection of Westminster Hall's 90ft (27m) high roof.

Facts and figures: The Palace is built on a 10ft (3m) thick bed of concrete, covers an area of five acres (20,200 square metres), has 1,100 rooms, 100 staircases, and 2 miles (3.2km) of corridors. The Palace was constructed with about 775,000 cubic feet (21,950 cubic metres) of Anston stone from Yorkshire. Over 300 statues decorate the main façades, representing saints and the sovereigns of England from the Saxon kings to Queen Victoria, many of them life size.

Decoration

Pugin was responsible for designing much of the interior decoration and many of the fittings in the Palace. Many examples of its tiles, metalwork, furniture, wallpaper and textiles are works of art in their own right. Pugin enlisted the help of three main collaborators: Herbert Minton (1793-1858), John Hardman (1811-67) and John Gregory Crace (1809-89).

The floor tiles used throughout the Palace are encaustic tiles, which means that different colours of clay are used to make the pattern and the design is more durable than it would be if another method were used. Pugin designed the tile schemes and Herbert Minton, a second-generation ceramics manufacturer from Stoke-on-Trent, developed the process for making them. The technique requires the tiles to be built up from as many as five layers of different coloured clay using a mould for each pattern, pouring in the clay, and firing the tile after each new layer is applied.

John Hardman of Birmingham made the stained glass windows and brasswork throughout the Palace to Pugin's designs. Hardman, a descendant of cast-metal manufacturers, had started his own business making brass buttons, but his friend Pugin persuaded him to enter into larger scale brass casting and stained glass manufacture. The scale of the metalwork varies widely from the brass gates at the entrance to the House of Lords, to the railing around the Lords Chamber and the door grilles and ink stands in the Library.

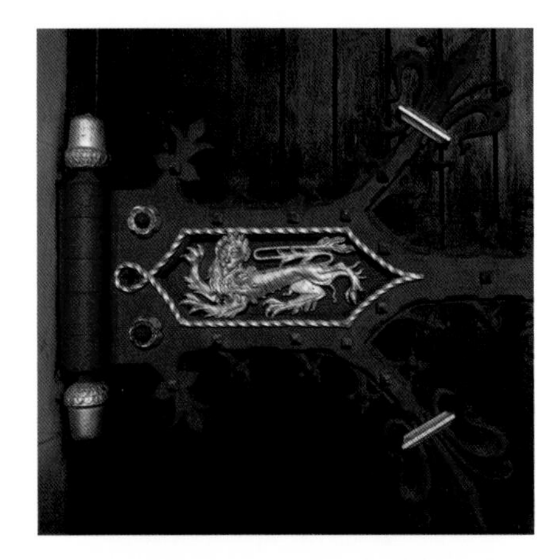

Patterns in the Palace's decoration include the lion rampant of Scotland (top), Welsh dragon (middle), lion passant representing England (left) and harp and shamrock, Ireland (bottom).

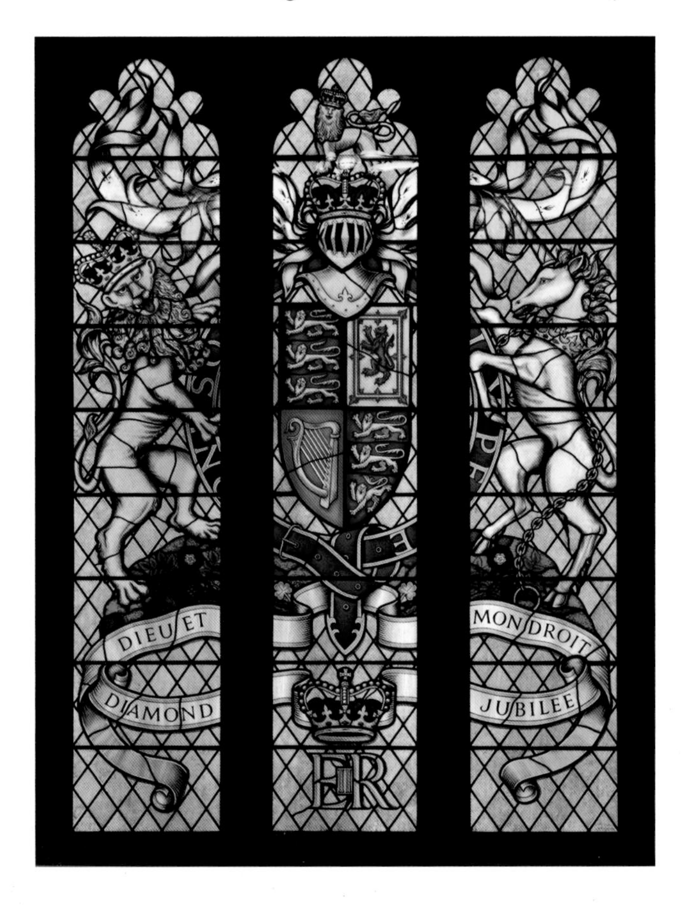

This stained glass window, showing the royal coat of arms, is a gift from the Members of both Houses to Her Majesty the Queen for the Diamond Jubilee.

The window was designed and made by the British artist John Reyntiens, who worked with a dedicated team. The design is a modern vision of a heraldic window. It takes its inspiration from 17th century heraldic art and the UK's long tradition of stained glass.

Pugin's third principal associate was John Gregory Crace, the third generation of his family to run an important decorating firm which also worked on Buckingham Palace and the Royal Pavilion in Brighton. Crace carried out all the painted decoration in the Palace – the stencilled ceilings and walls – and supplied wallpaper, curtain fabrics and some furniture. The wallpapers throughout the Palace were designed by Pugin in vivid colours and strong designs, including heraldic patterns, formal geometry and floral motifs. Some papers are flocks – patterns with a raised velvet-like texture. The papers were 'hand-blocked' using a block of wood (usually pear, box or holly) about 1ft 8in (50cm) square in which the pattern was carved. The blocks were covered in a special paint called distemper. They were carefully and repeatedly lowered on to plain strips of paper to form the pattern. The technique is still used today when new paper is required, as are the original blocks dating from the 1840s and 1850s.

Pugin, who was originally a furniture designer, designed most of the diverse collection of furniture, including chairs, tables and wardrobes. Some is still used, for example the chairs and octagonal tables in the Prince's Chamber (see below), and the Table in the Lords Chamber. After his death, the designs were copied or provided inspiration for many pieces of furniture made for the Palace.

Pugin designed this 'x-framed' chair which is one of two placed on either side of the Throne in the Lords Chamber.

The carved, painted and gilded royal motif of a crowned Tudor rose decorates doorways in the Royal Gallery.

Wallpapers in the Palace are hand-made using wooden blocks from hard woods such as pear or holly.

Parliamentary Archives

The Parliamentary Archives has custody of the records of both Houses of Parliament. The records, which are stored in the Victoria Tower, date from 1497, although most of the House of Commons' early records were lost in the 1834 fire. Earlier parliamentary records are held by the National Archives at Kew.

The records, which may be consulted by the public, include approximately 60,000 Acts of Parliament, the journals of both Houses, papers laid before Parliament, evidence and plans deposited in connection with private Bills and a wide range of administrative, ceremonial and architectural records. In addition there are over 200 other collections, the best known being the papers of David Lloyd George (1863-1945), Lord Beaverbrook (1879-1964) and Andrew Bonar Law (1858-1923).

Some of the most famous constitutional records of the United Kingdom are held by the Archives. These include five documents which are inscribed on the UNESCO Memory of the World UK Register: the Death Warrant of Charles I (1649), the Bill of Rights (1689), the Women's Freedom League banner which was unfurled in the House of Commons in 1908, the Prisoners (Temporary Discharge for Ill-health) Act 1913 (known as the Cat and Mouse Act) and the Representation of the People (Equal Franchise) Act 1928.

The archives contain many other important documents. The Petition of Right (1628) which proclaimed that it was illegal to impose taxation without Parliament's consent is there, as are the Articles of Union between England and Scotland (1706). There is the Stamp Act (1765) which imposed taxes on legal documents and other goods and services in the American colonies. This contributed to a growing resistance to British rule and the eventual outbreak of the American revolutionary war in 1775. The archives also contain the Act to abolish the British slave trade (1807) and the Great Reform Act (1832), which abolished rotten boroughs – constituencies with only a few voters that sent MPs to Parliament. The Parliament Act of 1911, which established the supremacy of the Commons over the Lords, is another document of constitutional significance.

An Act declaring the Rights and Liberties of the Subject, and settling the Succession of the Crown *(the 'Bill of Rights'), 1 William & Mary Session 2, c. 2, 1689.*
Parliamentary Archives, HL/PO/PU/1/1688/1W&MS1N2

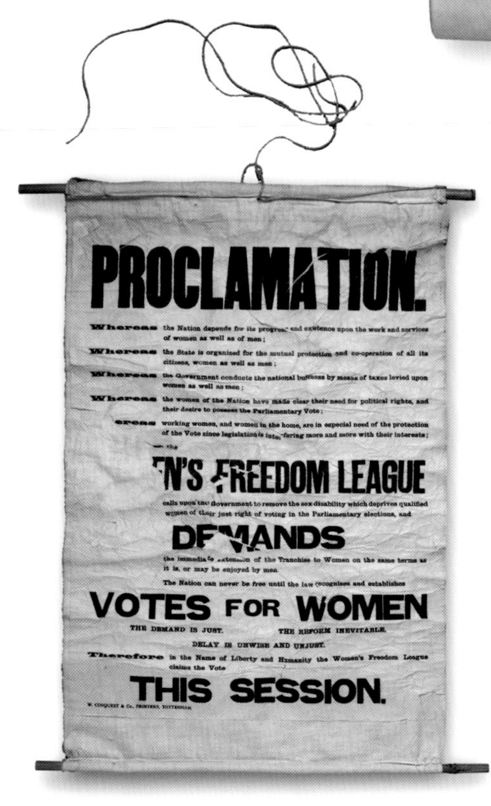

Suffragette banner, 28 October 1908.
Parliamentary Archives, HC/SA/SJ/3/1

Prisoners (Temporary Discharge for Ill-Health) Act, c. 4, 1913.
Parliamentary Archives, HL/PO/PU/1/1913/3&4G5c4

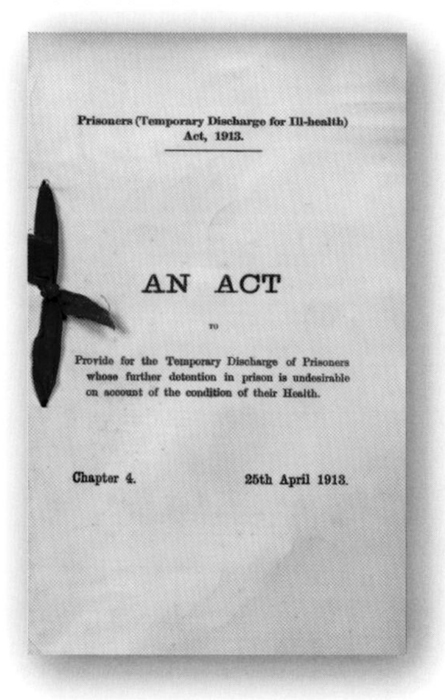

Prisoners (Temporary Discharge for Ill-health) Act, 1913.

AN ACT

TO

Provide for the Temporary Discharge of Prisoners whose further detention in prison is undesirable on account of the condition of their Health.

Chapter 4. 25th April 1913.

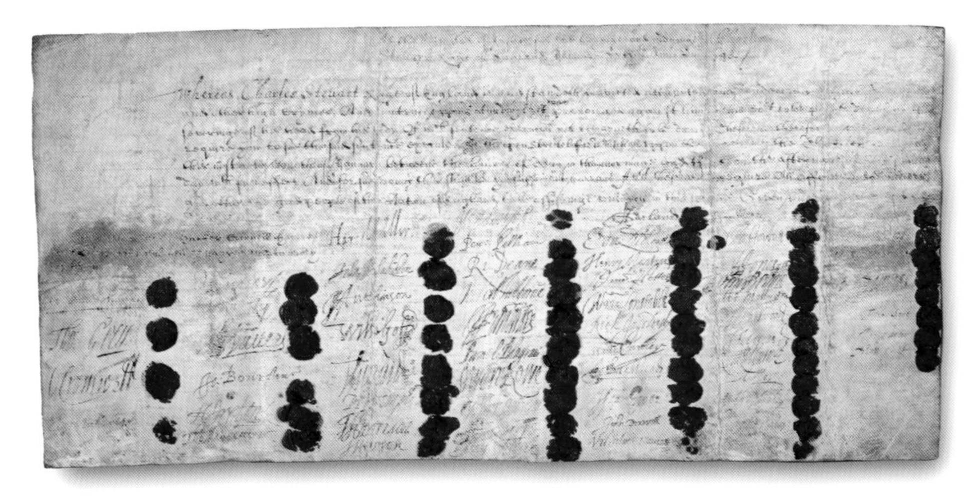

Death Warrant of King Charles I, *29 January 1649*.
Parliamentary Archives, HL/PO/JO/10/1/297A

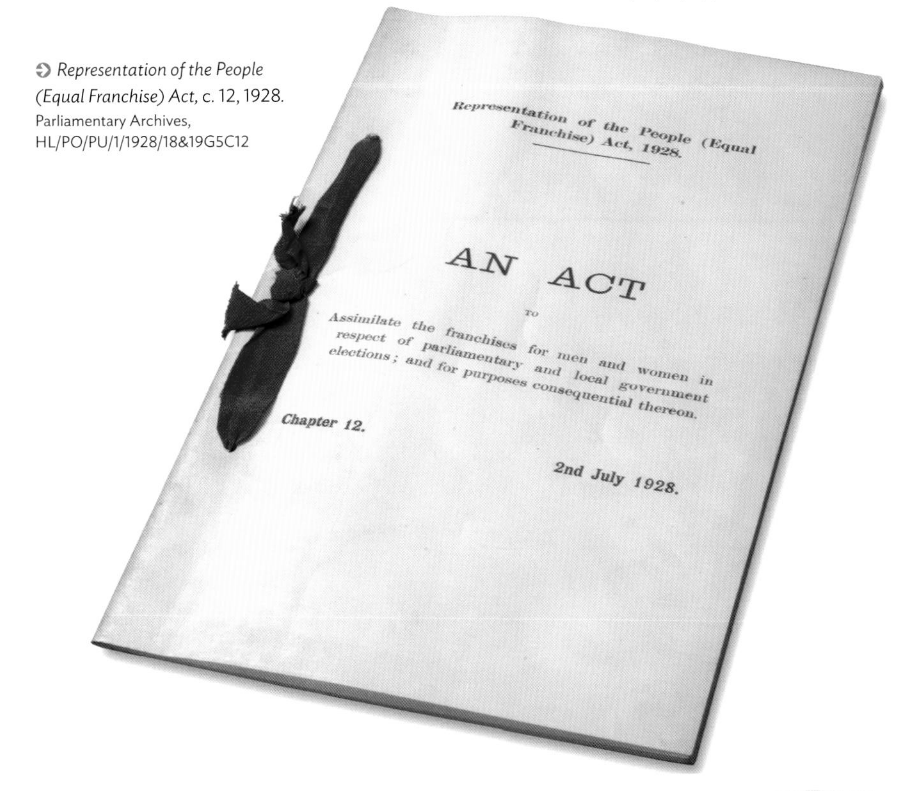

Representation of the People (Equal Franchise) Act, 1928.

AN ACT

TO

Assimilate the franchises for men and women in respect of parliamentary and local government elections; and for purposes consequential thereon.

Chapter 12.

2nd July 1928.

Representation of the People (Equal Franchise) Act, c. 12, 1928.
Parliamentary Archives, HL/PO/PU/1/1928/18&19G5C12

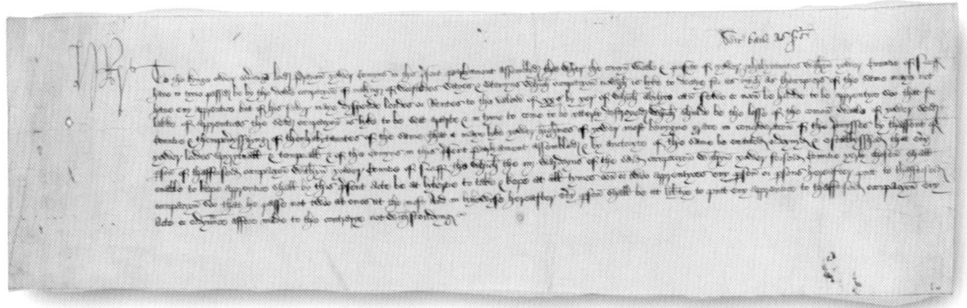

An Act for taking of Apprentices to make Worsteds in the County of Norfolk, 12 Henry VII, c.1, 1497. The earliest parliamentary document held by the Archives.
Parliamentary Archives, HL/PO/PU/1/1497/12H7N1

Acts are all on parchment (animal skin) – a material chosen because of its long-lasting qualities. The Acts are rolls up to 1849, and thereafter in book form.

Also to be found in the collections of the Parliamentary Archives

The Longest Act, estimated to be 348m unrolled, which was passed in 1821 and appointed commissioners to collect the Land Tax.
Land Tax Act, 1 & 2 George IV, c. 123, 1821.
Parliamentary Archives, HL/PO/PU/1/1821/1&2G4N248

Plans for roads, canals and railways built in the United Kingdom from 1794 onwards. These have been submitted to Parliament with the Private Bills required to authorise their construction.
Parliamentary Archives, HL/PO/PB/3, HC/CL/PB/6

A specimen of an oil slick from the wrecked tanker *Eleni V*, which was given as evidence in 1978 to a House of Commons Select Committee on Science and Technology inquiry into contingency arrangements for dealing with oil pollution.
Parliamentary Archives, HC/CP/4417

A tombstone fragment which was submitted as evidence by James Tracy in 1845 to support his claim to be Viscount Tracy of Rathcoole and sit in the House of Lords. We will never know whether the tombstone would have made it possible for Tracy to become a Member of the House of Lords as he died before a decision was reached.
Tombstone fragment, Parliamentary Archives, HL/PO/DC/CP/3/105A

Rt Hon. Margaret Beckett MP
Antony Williams, tempera on board, 2011 [WOA 7203]

Parliamentary Art

The Parliamentary Art Collection includes over 8,000 works of art, most of which are displayed in the Palace of Westminster and other parliamentary buildings. The Collection's paintings, sculptures and other artworks illustrate the history of Parliament and British politics over the centuries.

The earliest works in the Collection are 14th century gothic statues of kings in Westminster Hall. Images of leading parliamentarians are a key part of the Collection, and there are images of monarchs and group portraits which record historic events in the two Chambers. The buildings of the Palace of Westminster and the parliamentary estate are also well represented. Drawings and watercolours chart the buildings' evolution through the 17th, 18th and early 19th centuries. The dramatic fire of 1834, the construction of the new Palace of Westminster and more recent buildings like Portcullis House all feature.

Many of the larger works were commissioned for the new Palace of Westminster in the 19th century. Since 1990, Works of Art Committees in the House of Commons and House of Lords have enriched the contemporary collection by promoting the work of living artists. In particular, by acquiring work by artists from the United Kingdom's different regions, they have brought together images from around the country.

William Cowper, first Lord Chancellor of Britain (following Act of Union)
Thomas Murray, oil on canvas, c. 1695 [WOA 6181]

Charles Abbot, Speaker 1802-17
Thomas Lawrence, oil on canvas, 1824 [WOA 2715]

Rev. Dr Ian Paisley MP
Mark Shields, oil on canvas, 2008 [WOA 7028]

Earl of Rosebery ceramic teapot
Shelley Foley from the 'Intarsio' range, 20th century [WOA S636]

Women's Social and Political Union medal awarded to Emmeline Pankhurst in 1908, silver [WOA M0564]

Flux
Diane Ibbotson, oil on canvas, 1998–2000 [WOA 7200]

Rt Hon. The Baroness Amos
Paul Benney, oil on canvas, 2004 [WOA 6386]

Horseguards Parade (No 5)
Robert Tavener, linocut, 1967 [WOA 7049]

Works of Art on the Tour

Unless otherwise stated, paintings are oil on canvas and sculpture is marble.
Works are listed clockwise from point of entry on the tour route.

SOVEREIGN'S ENTRANCE LOBBY

Sculpture

John Wodehouse, 1st Earl of Kimberley (1826-1902), Liberal Party leader, by William Hamo Thornycroft, 1908 WOAS54

George Douglas Campbell, 8th Duke of Argyll (1823-1900), Lord Privy Seal, by George James Frampton, 1908 WOAS5

NORMAN PORCH

Paintings

Queen Victoria (1819-1901), by W A Menzies after Benjamin Constant, 1924 WOA3156

Edward 1st Baron Thurlow (1731-1816) Lord Chancellor, by George Romney, c. 1784 WOA5404

Sculpture

Alexander Frederick Douglas-Home, Lord Home of the Hirsel (1903-95), Prime Minister, by Michael Black, 1982 WOAS125

Charles Grey, 2nd Earl Grey (1764-1845), Prime Minister, by Thomas Campbell, 1827 WOAS44

William Pitt the Elder, 1st Earl of Chatham (1708-78), Prime Minister, by Joseph Wilton, 1780 WOAS21

Arthur Wellesley, 1st Duke of Wellington (1769-1852), Prime Minister 1828-30, by Edward Hodges Baily, 19th century WOAS90

William Lamb, 2nd Viscount Melbourne (1779-1848), Prime Minister, by unknown artist, no date WOAS198

George Hamilton Gordon, 4th Earl of Aberdeen (1784-1860), Prime Minister, by V d'Alessandro after Matthew Noble (1874), 1964 WOAS1

Edward Geoffrey Stanley, 14th Earl of Derby (1799-1869), Prime Minister, by Feodora Gleichen, 1892 WOAS31

Benjamin Disraeli, 1st Earl of Beaconsfield (1804-81), Prime Minister, by Count Gleichen, 1880 WOAS12

Charles Watson-Wentworth, 2nd Marquess of Rockingham (1730-82), Prime Minister, by Joseph Nollekens, 1782 WOAS75

Henry Addington, 1st Viscount Sidmouth (1757-1844), Prime Minister, by William Behnes, 1831 WOALS30

Henry John Temple, 3rd Viscount Palmerston (1784-1865), Prime Minister, after Matthew Noble, no date WOAS124

Archibald Philip Primrose, 5th Earl of Rosebery (1847-1929), Prime Minister, by V d'Alessandro after Sir Joseph Boehm (1886), 1963 WOAS76

Robert Arthur Gascoyne-Cecil, 3rd Marquess Salisbury (1830-1903), Prime Minister, by William Theed, 1875 WOALS32

Robert Banks Jenkinson, 2nd Earl of Liverpool (1770-1828), Prime Minister, Joseph Nollekens, 1816 WOAS197

William Wyndham 1st Baron Grenville (1759-1834), Prime Minister, by Joseph Nollekens, c. 1800 WOALS35

ROBING ROOM

Paintings

Queen Victoria (1819-1901), after Franz Xaver Winterhalter (1859), no date WOA3154

Francis Charles Augustus Emmanuel Albert (1819-61), Prince Consort of Queen Victoria, after Franz Xaver Winterhalter (1859), no date WOA3155

The Legend of King Arthur, by William Dyce, frescoes, commissioned 1848, completed 1866:

- *Hospitality: Admission of Sir Tristram to the Round Table,* unfinished by Dyce, completed by Charles West Cope from 1864-66 WOA3153
- *Mercy: Sir Gawaine swearing to be merciful* WOA3152
- *Courtesy: Sir Tristram harping to La Beale Isoude* WOA3151
- *Religion: The Vision of Sir Galahad and His Company* WOA3149
- *Generosity: King Arthur unhorsed spared by Sir Launcelot* WOA3150

Sculpture

The Legend of King Arthur, by H H Armstead, oak reliefs, 1866:

- *King Arthur carried in a Barge to Avillon attended by Queens* WOAS117
- *Sir Mordred slaine King Arthur wounded to death* WOAS116
- *The Misadventure of the Adder – beginning the Battaile* WOAS115
- *The Knights of the Round Table vowing to seek the Sancgreall* WOAS114
- *King Arthur conquering the marvailous Gyant* WOAS113
- *King Arthur wedded to Guenever* WOAS112
- *How Arthur gate his Sword Excalibur* WOAS111
- *The Battaile with King Lot* WOAS110
- *Arthur crowned King* WOAS109
- *Arthur recognized as King* WOAS108
- *Arthur delivered unto Merlin* WOAS107
- *The Birth of King Arthur* WOAS106
- *Sir Galahad's Soul borne to Heaven* WOAS123
- *Sir Galahad imprisoned by the Tyrant* WOAS122
- *Sir Galahad, Sir Percivale, Sir Bors* WOAS121
- *Receives the sword with the strange girdels* WOAS120
- *Sir Galahad brought unto the Siege perillous* WOAS119
- *Sir Launcelot leaving Dame Elaine* WOAS118

Her Majesty Queen Elizabeth II, by Oscar Nemon, bronze, cast 2008 WOAS527

ROYAL GALLERY

Paintings

George I (1660-1727), by Sir Godfrey Kneller, no date WOA3162

George II (1683-1760), after Sir Godfrey Kneller, no date WOA3160

Elizabeth II (b 1926), Queen Regnant, by Sir James Gunn, commissioned 1954 WOA3161

George VI (1895-1952), by Robert Swan after Sir Gerald Kelly, 1945 WOA3159

George V (1865-1936), by Sir Luke Fildes, no date WOA3158

Edward VII (1841-1910), after Sir Luke Fildes, WOA3173

William IV (1765-1837), attributed to Sir William Beechey, 1831-2 WOA3171

George III (1738-1820), after Sir Joshua Reynolds, 1779, WOA3172

George IV (1762-1830), after Sir Thomas Lawrence, WOA3170

Adelaide Amelia Louisa Theresa Carolina (1792-1849), Queen of William IV, attributed to Sir William Beechey, 1831-2 WOA3169

Charlotte of Mecklenburg-Strelitz (1744-1818), Queen of George III, after Sir Joshua Reynolds, no date WOA3168

Alexandra of Denmark (1844-1925), by Sir Luke Fildes, no date WOA3167

Queen Mary (1867-1953), Macbeth-Raeburn after Sir William Llewellyn, 1918 WOA3166

Elizabeth, Queen Mother (1900-2002), by Robert Swan after Sir Gerald Kelly, no date WOA3165

Queen Caroline (1683-1737), Queen of George II, after Sir Godfrey Kneller, no date WOA3163

Prince Philip, Duke of Edinburgh (b 1921), by A C Davidson-Houston, 1971 WOA3164

Wall Paintings

The Death of Nelson Supported by Captain Hardy on the Victory at Battle of Trafalgar, by Daniel Maclise, Waterglass on plaster, 1866 WOA3247

The Death of Nelson, C W Sharpe after D Maclise, engraving, published by the Art-Union of London, 1876 WOA4164

The Meeting of Wellington and Blucher After the Battle of Waterloo, by Daniel Maclise, Waterglass on plaster, 1861 WOA3246

The Meeting of Wellington and Blucher after the Battle of Waterloo, Lumb Stocks after Daniel Maclise, engraving, 1872 WOA4159

Sculpture

Warrior Kings & Queens, by John Birnie Philip, gilt Caen stone, 1869:

Elizabeth I (1533-1603) WOAS34
William III (1650-1702) WOAS92
Queen Anne (1665-1714) WOAS4
Alfred the Great (849-901) WOAS2
William I the Conqueror (1027-87) WOAS91
Richard I (1157-99) WOAS73
Edward III (1312-77) WOAS33
Henry V (1387-1422) WOAS48

PRINCE'S CHAMBER

Paintings

Tudor Portraits, Royal School of Art students under direction of Richard Burchett, oil on panel, 1854-60:

King Louis XII of France (1462-1515) WOA3200
Princess Mary (1496-1533) WOA3201
Charles Brandon, 1st Duke of Suffolk (d 1545) WOA3202
Frances, Marchioness of Dorset (1517-59) WOA3203
Lady Jane Grey (1537-54), Queen 1553 WOA3204
Lord Guildford Dudley (d 1554) WOA3205
King James IV of Scotland (1473-1513) WOA3206
Princess Margaret, Queen of Scotland (1489-1541) WOA3207
Archibald Douglas, Earl of Angus (d 1557) WOA3208
King James V of Scotland (1512-42) WOA3209
Mary of Guise, Queen of Scotland (1515-60) WOA3210
Mary Queen of Scots (1542-87) WOA3211
King Francis II of France (1544-60) WOA3212
Henry Lord Darnley (1545-67) WOA3213
Henry VII (1457-1509) WOA3186
Queen Elizabeth of York (1465-1503) WOA3187
Arthur Prince of Wales (1486-1502) WOA3188
Queen Catherine of Aragon (1485-1536) WOA3189
King Henry VIII (1491-1547) WOA3190
Queen Anne Boleyn (1507-36) WOA3191
Queen Jane Seymour (1509-37) WOA3192
Queen Anne of Cleves (1515-57) WOA3193
Queen Catherine Howard (d 1542) WOA3194
Queen Catherine Parr (1512-48) WOA3195
King Edward VI (1537-53) WOA3196
Queen Mary I (1516-58) WOA3197
King Philip II of Spain and I of England (1527-98) WOA3198
Queen Elizabeth I (1553-1603) WOA3199

The Armada Series, one canvas by Richard Burchett, c. 1860s, five canvases by Anthony Oakshett, 2010:

The Sharpest Engagement against the Isle of Wight WOA7126
English Fireships Dislodge the Spanish Fleet before Calais WOA7127
The Discovery of the Spanish Fleet opposite the Lizard WOA7123
The English Fleet Pursuing the Spanish Fleet Against Fowey by Burchett WOA2954
Drake takes De Valdes's Galleon, The Lord Admiral Pursues the Enemy WOA7124
The Engagement of Both Fleets against the Isle of Portland WOA7125

Sculpture

Queen Victoria and supporting figures of Justice & Clemency by John Gibson, 1855 WOAS88

Episodes from Tudor History, by William Theed, bronze, 1856:

Mary Queen of Scots looking back on France WOAS98
The Escape of Mary Queen of Scots WOAS96
The Murder of Rizzio WOAS97
The Visit of the Emperor Charles V to Henry VIII WOAS95
Edward VI granting a Charter to Christ's Hospital WOAS102
Lady Jane Grey at her Studies WOAS103
Sebastian Cabot before Henry VII WOAS104
Catherine of Aragon pleading WOAS105
The Field of the Cloth of Gold WOAS94
Raleigh spreading his Cloak as a Carpet for the Queen WOAS100
Queen Elizabeth I knighting Sir Francis Drake WOAS99
The Death of Sir Philip Sidney WOAS101

HOUSE OF LORDS CHAMBER

Fresco paintings

(above the throne left to right as viewed)

Edward III Conferring the Order of the Garter on the Black Prince, by Charles West Cope, 1848 WOA2965

The Baptism of King Ethelbert, by William Dyce, 1846 WOA2964

Prince Henry Acknowledging the authority of Chief Justice Gascoigne, by Charles West Cope, 1849 WOA2966

(opposite thrown left to right as viewed)

Spirit of Justice, by Daniel Maclise, 1849 WOA2967

Spirit of Religion, by J C Horsley, 1847 WOA2968

Spirit of Chivalry, by Daniel Maclise, 1848 WOA2969

Sculpture

Magna Carta Barons, gilt metal, completed 1858 (clockwise starting right of throne):

Henri de Londres, Archbishop of Dublin (d 1228), by John Thomas WOAS56
William Marshal, Earl of Pembroke (c 1146-1219), by John E Thomas WOAS67
Almeric, Master of the Knights Templar, by Patrick MacDowell WOAS3
William de Warenne, Earl of Surrey (d 1240), by Patrick MacDowell WOAS84
William D'Aubigny, Earl of Sussex and Arundel (d 1221), by W F Woodington WOAS6
Hubert de Burgh, Earl of Kent (d 1243), by W F Woodington WOAS53
Richard de Clare, Earl of Hertford (d 1217), by Henry Timbrell WOAS50
William de Forz, Count of Aumale, Lord of Holderness (d 1241), Henry Timbrell & J S Westmacott WOAS7
Geoffrey de Mandeville, Earl of Essex & Gloucester (d 1215), by J S Westmacott WOAS40
Saher de Quency, Earl of Winchester (d 1219), by J S Westmacott WOAS93
Henry de Bohun, Earl of Hereford (d 1220), by T Thornycroft WOAS49
Roger le Bigod, Earl of Norfolk (d 1221), by T Thornycroft WOAS61
Robert de Vere, Earl of Oxford (c 1164-1221), by Frederick Thrupp WOAS63

Robert Fitzwalter (d 1235), by Frederick Thrupp WOAS37
Eustace de Vescy (c 1170-1216), by A H Ritchie WOAS86
William de Mowbray (d 1223), by A H Ritchie WOAS60
William Longespee, Earl of Salisbury (d 1225), by John E Thomas WOAS78
Stephen Langton, Archbishop of Canterbury (d 1228), by John Thomas WOAS55

PEERS CORRIDOR

Paintings

'Civil War' paintings by Charles West Cope, 1856-65:

The Burial of Charles I at Windsor 1649, fresco WOA2895
The Expulsion of the Fellows of a College at Oxford for Refusing to Sign the Covenant 1647, waterglass WOA2896
Basing House defended by the Cavaliers against the Parliamentary Army 1645, waterglass WOA2897
Charles I Raising His Standard at Nottingham 1642, fresco WOA2898
Speaker Lenthall Asserting the Privileges of the Commons against Charles I when the Attempt was made to Seize the Five Members 1642, waterglass WOA2894
The Setting Out of the Train Bands from London to Raise the Siege of Gloucester 1643, waterglass WOA2893
The Embarkation of the Pilgrim Fathers for New England 1620, fresco WOA2892
The Parting of Lord and Lady Russell 1683, fresco WOA2891

CENTRAL LOBBY

Mosaic

St George for England by Sir E J Poynter PRA, 1870 WOA4257
St Patrick for Ireland by Robert Anning Bell RA, 1924 WOA4254
St David for Wales by Sir E J Poynter PRA, 1898 WOA4255
St Andrew for Scotland by Robert Anning Bell RA, 1923 WOA4256

Sculpture

George Leveson-Gower, 2nd Earl Granville (1815-91), by Hamo Thornycroft, 1895 WOAS42
William Ewart Gladstone (1809-98), Prime Minister, by F W Pomeroy, 1900 WOAS39
Sir Stafford Henry Northcote, 1st Earl of Iddesleigh (1817-87) Foreign Secretary, by Sir Joseph Boehm, 1888 WOAS52
Lord John 1st Earl Russell (1792-1878) Prime Minister, by Sir Joseph Boehm, 1880 WOAS77

Royal Ancestry statues by John Thomas & the Thames Bank Workshop, commissioned 1837, complete by 1854, stone

West Entrance (to St Stephen's Hall)

Edward I (1239-1307) WOAS149
Eleanor of Castille, Queen of Edward I WOAS150
Edward II (1284-1327) WOAS151
Isabella, second Queen of Richard II WOAS152
Henry III (1207-72) WOAS153
Eleanor of Provence, Queen of Henry III WOAS154

North West side

Henry VIII (1491-1547) WOAS173
Anne Boleyn, second Queen of Henry VIII WOAS174
Edward VI (1537-53) WOAS175
Mary I (1516-58) WOAS176
Elizabeth I (1533-1603) WOAS177
James I of England & VI of Scotland (1566-1625) WOAS178

North Entrance (to Commons Corridor)

Isabella of France, Queen of Edward II WOAS155
Henry IV (1367-1413) WOAS156
Edward III (1312-77) WOAS157
Richard II (1367-1400) WOAS158
Anne of Bohemia, Queen of Richard II WOAS159
Philippa of Hainault, Queen of Edward III WOAS160

North East side

Anne of Denmark, Queen of James I WOAS179
Charles I (1600-49) WOAS180
Henrietta Maria, Queen of Charles I WOAS181
Charles II (1630-85) WOAS182
James II (1633-1701) WOAS183
Anne Hyde, 1st wife of James II WOAS184

East Entrance

Joan of Navarre, Queen of Henry IV WOAS161
Henry V (1387-1422) WOAS162
Catherine of France, Queen of Henry V WOAS163
Henry VI (1421-71) WOAS164
Margaret of Anjou, Queen of Henry VI WOAS165
Edward IV (1442-83) WOAS166

South East side

William III (1650-1702) WOAS185
Mary II (1662-94), Queen of William III WOAS186
Anne (1665-1714) WOAS187
George I (1660-1727) WOAS188
Sophia of Zell, Queen of George I WOAS189
George II (1683-1760) WOAS190

COMMONS CORRIDOR

Paintings

'Glorious Revolution' paintings by Edward M Ward, commissioned 1853, completed 1868:

Alice Lisle Concealing the Fugitives after the Battle of Sedgemoor, fresco WOA2604
The Last Sleep of Argyll, fresco WOA2605
The Lords and Commons Presenting the Crown to William and Mary in the Banqueting House 1688, waterglass WOA2606
The Acquittal of the Seven Bishops, waterglass WOA2607
General Monk Declaring for a Free Parliament 1660, waterglass WOA2608
The Landing of Charles II at Dover 1660, waterglass WOA2609
The Executioner Tying Wisharts Book Round the Neck of Montrose, fresco WOA2610
Charles II Assisted in His Escape by Jane Lane, waterglass WOA2611

MEMBERS LOBBY

Sculpture

Statues of Prime Ministers (clockwise from statue of Margaret Thatcher):

Baroness Margaret Thatcher (born 1925) by Antony Dufort, bronze, 2007 WOAS531
Herbert Henry Asquith, 1st Earl of Oxford & Asquith (1852-1928) by Leonard Merrifield (1939-43) completed Gilbert Bayes (1948), WOAS64
Arthur James, 1st Earl of Balfour (1848-1930) by David McFall, Larrys Roche stone, 1962 WOAS8
Sir Winston Leonard Spencer Churchill (1874-1964) by Oscar Nemon, bronze, 1969 WOAS23
David, 1st Earl Lloyd George (1863-1945) by Uli Nimptsch, bronze, 1963 WOAS57
Benjamin Disraeli, 1st Earl of Beaconsfield (1804-81), by Count Gleichen, 1883 WOAS11
Clement Richard, 1st Earl Attlee, Viscount Prestwood (1883-1967) by Ivor Roberts-Jones, bronze, 1976 WOAS69

Portrait busts of Prime Ministers (clockwise from statue of Margaret Thatcher):
Sir Edward Heath (1916-2005) by Martin Jennings, bronze, 1993 WOAS234
Sir Alec Douglas-Home (1903-95) by Angela Conner, bronze, 2006 WOAS528
James Callaghan (1912-2005) by Ian Walters, bronze 2002 WOAS517
Maurice Harold Macmillan, 1st Earl of Stockton, Viscount Macmillan of Ovenden (1894-1986), by Oscar Nemon, bronze, 1959 WOAS257
Sir John Major (born 1943), by Anne Curry, bronze 2007 WOAS529
Sir Henry Campbell Bannerman (1836-1908), by Martin Jennings, bronze, 2009 WOAS691
Andrew Bonar Law (1858-1923), cast from original by John E. Hyett, bronze, 2008 WOAS689
James Ramsay MacDonald (1866-1937), by Jacob Epstein, bronze, 1934 WOAS222
Rt Hon. Neville Chamberlain (1869-1940), by Lady Kathleen Kennet, bronze, 1936, on loan from Birmingham Museums and Art Gallery WOALS40
Stanley Baldwin, 1st Earl Baldwin of Bewdley (1867-1947), by Newbury A Trent, bronze, 1927, on loan to Palace of Westminster WOALS1
Sir Anthony Eden, 1st Lord Avon (1897-1977), by Roy Noakes, bronze, 1994 WOAS235
Harold Wilson (1916-95), by Ian Walters, bronze, 2000 WOAS512

ST STEPHEN'S HALL

Paintings

Building of Britain wall paintings, commissioned 1925 completed by 1927:
Sir Thomas More Refusing to Grant Wolsey a Subsidy, 1523 by Vivian Forbes, WOA2596
Queen Elizabeth Commissions Raleigh to Sail for America, 1584 by Alfred K Lawrence, WOA2597
Sir Thomas Roe at the Court of Ajmir, 1614 by Sir William Rothenstein, WOA2598
The Parliamentary Union of England and Scotland, 1707 by Walter T Monnington, WOA2599
King Alfred's Long-Ships Defeat the Danes, 877 by Colin Gill, WOA2600
Richard I Leaving England for the Crusades, 1189 by Glyn W Philpot WOA2601
King John Assents to Magna Carta 1215 by Charles Sims, WOA2602
The English People Reading Wycliffe's Bible by Sir George Clausen, WOA2603

Mosaics by Robert Anning Bell RA
St Stephen, King Stephen and King Edward the Confessor, 1925 WOA4258
King Edward III commands the rebuilding of St Stephen's Chapel, 1926 WOA4259

Sculpture

Statues of statesmen, commissioned 1845 completed 1858:
John Hampden (1594-1643) by J H Foley WOAS45
John Selden (1584-1654) by J H Foley WOAS80
Sir Robert Walpole, 1st Earl of Orford (1676-1745) by John Bell WOAS62
William Pitt, 1st Earl of Chatham (1708-78) by Patrick MacDowell WOAS19
William Pitt (1759-1806) by Patrick MacDowell WOAS70
Henry Grattan (1746-1820) by John Edward Carew WOAS43
Edmund Burke (1729-97) by William Theed WOAS16
Charles James Fox (1749-1806) by E H Baily WOAS38
William Murray, 1st Earl of Mansfield (1705-93) by E H Baily WOAS58
John, 1st Baron Somers (1651-1716) by William Calder Marshall WOAS82
Lucius Cary, 2nd Viscount Falkland (1610-43) by John Bell WOAS35
Edward Hyde, 1st Earl of Clarendon (1609-74) by William Calder Marshall WOAS25

Royal Ancestry statues by John Thomas & the Thames Bank Workshop, commissioned 1837, complete c. 1854, stone

West Entrance to St Stephen's Porch
William I, The Conqueror (1027-87) WOAS137
Maude, Matilda of Flanders, Queen of William I WOAS138
William II (d.1100) WOAS139
Henry I (1068-1135) WOAS140
Matilda, First Queen of Henry I WOAS141
Stephen (1097-1154) WOAS142

East Entrance (to Central Lobby)
Matilda, Queen of Stephen WOAS143
Henry II (1133-89) WOAS144
Eleanor of Aquitaine Queen of Henry II WOAS145
Richard I (1157-99) WOAS146
Berengaria of Navarre, Queen of Richard I WOAS147
John (1167-1216) WOAS148

ST STEPHEN'S PORCH

Painting

Moses Receiving the Law on Mount Sinai by Benjamin West, 1784 WOA5215

Sculpture

First World War Memorial (the recording Angel flanked by two allegorical figures) by Bertram MacKennal, stone, 1921 WOAS220

WESTMINSTER HALL

Statues of Medieval kings, stone, WOAS126-136

South Wall
Six medieval kings by Thomas Canon, *c.* 1388

Window ledges
Five medieval kings formerly on exterior of building

TIME LINE

1000 1100 1200 1300 1400 1500 1600 1650

Palace of Westminster

c. **1016** King Canute begins building a residence

c. **1045** Palace is built by Edward the Confessor

1097-9 William Rufus builds Westminster Hall

c. **1220** Exchequer moves to Westminster from Winchester

1292-7 Edward I begins building St Stephen's Chapel and Chapel of St Mary Undercroft

1348 St Stephen's Chapel completed

c. **1365** Jewel Tower is built

1393-1401 Richard II rebuilds Westminster Hall in its present form

1503 Building starts on the Henry VII Chapel in Westminster Abbey

1512 Following a fire, the Palace ceases to be a royal residence

1526-9 Cloisters are built

1547 Commons starts to use St Stephen's Chapel as its Chamber. Lords sits in Queen's Chamber

William Rufus *(1056-1100, reigned 1087-1100)*

Richard II *(1367-1400, reigned 1377-99)*

Henry VIII *(1491-1547, reigned 1509-47)*

British parliamentary and constitutional history

1066 Norman Conquest of England by William I (the Conqueror)

1215 *Magna Carta*

1265 Simon de Montfort's Parliament

1305 Trial of William Wallace in Westminster Hall

1315 First Clerk of the Parliaments is appointed

1363 First Clerk of the Commons is appointed

1377 First known Speaker, Thomas Hungerford, is elected

1485 Henry VII accedes to the throne, the start of the Tudor dynasty

1536 Union between England and Wales

1542 First Welsh MPs in the Commons

1605 Gunpowder Plot

1628 *Petition of Right*

1642 Charles I tries to arrest the five MPs

1642-9 English Civil War

1649 Charles I execute

1653 Cromw expels Parliament

Major events

1100s Angkor Wat temple is built by Khmers

1185 Start of feudal epoch under Shoguns in Japan

Genghis Khan *(c. 1162-1227)*

1256 Hanseatic League is formed

Marco Polo *(1254-1324)*

1299 Ottoman Empire founded by Osman I

1368 Start of the Ming dynasty in China

1337-1453 Hundred Years War between England and France

c. **1440** Gutenberg's printing press

Leonardo da Vinci *(1452-1519)*

1400s-1500s Italian Renaissance

1492 Christopher Columbus lands in America

1501 Start of Safavid rule in Persia

1519 Cortés arrives in Mexico

1588 Spanish Armada

William Shakespeare *(1564-1616)*

Miguel de Cervantes *(1547-1616)*

1648 Peace of Westphalia ends Thirty Years War